GUIDE TO THE UNIVERSITY OF FLORIDA AND GAINESVILLE

Guide TO THE UNIVERSITY OF FLORIDA

Pineapple Press, Inc.
Sarasota, Florida

and
GAINESVILLE

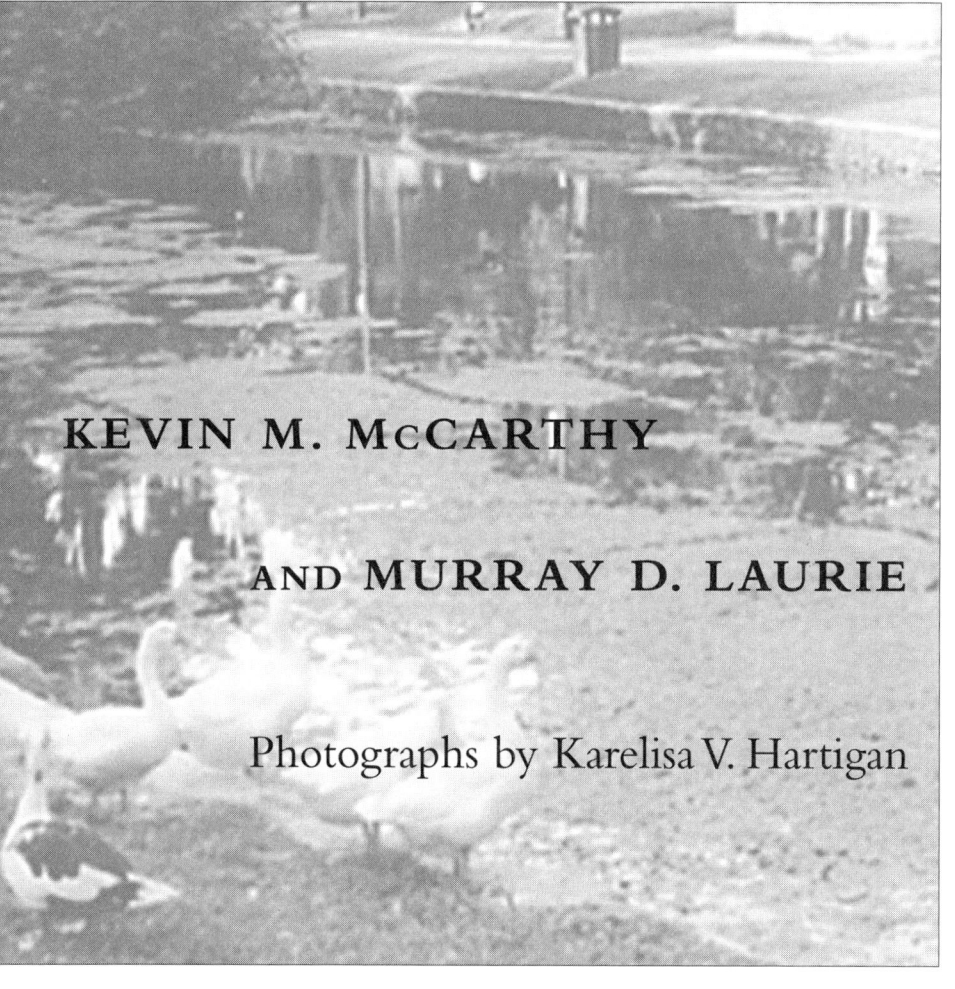

KEVIN M. McCARTHY

AND MURRAY D. LAURIE

Photographs by Karelisa V. Hartigan

Copyright © 1997 by Kevin M. McCarthy and Murray D. Laurie
Photographs Copyright © 1997 by Karelisa V. Hartigan unless otherwise credited

All rights reserved. No part of this book may be reproduced in any form or by any means, electronic or mechanical, including photocopying, recording, or by any information storage and retrieval system, without permission in writing from the publisher.

Inquiries should be addressed to:
Pineapple Press, Inc.
P.O. Box 3899
Sarasota, Florida 34230

Library of Congress Cataloging in Publication Data
McCarthy, Kevin M., 1940–
      Guide to the University of Florida and Gainesville / by Kevin M. McCarthy and Murray D. Laurie. — 1st ed.
         p.   cm.
      Includes bibliographical references and index.
      ISBN 1-56164-134-0 (pbk. : alk. paper)
    1. University of Florida. 2. University of Florida—Pictorial works. 3. Gainesville (Fla.)—Description and travel. 4. Gainesville (Fla.)—Pictorial works. I. Laurie, Murray D. II. Title.
LD1794.L38   1997   97-30139
378.759'75—dc21   CIP

First Edition
10 9 8 7 6 5 4 3 2 1

Design by Carol Tornatore
Printed and bound by Edwards Brothers, Lillington, North Carolina

CONTENTS

INTRODUCTION   ix

PART ONE: GAINESVILLE   1

SHORT HISTORY OF ALACHUA COUNTY   3

SHORT HISTORY OF GAINESVILLE   7

DOWNTOWN GAINESVILLE   10

- I.   EAST UNIVERSITY AVENUE   13 (Map on page 12)

- II.   SOUTHEAST DISTRICT   29 (Map on page 30)
  1st Avenue 31, 1st Street 38, 2nd Avenue 39, 2nd Place 42, 7th Street 43, 7th Avenue 46, 12th Street 47, 15th Street 48, 21st Avenue 49

- III.   SOUTH MAIN STREET and SOUTHWEST DISTRICT   51 (Map on page 52)
  South Main Street 53, 1st Avenue 59, 2nd Avenue 60, 2nd Place 63, Depot Avenue 64

- IV.   NORTH MAIN STREET and NORTHEAST DISTRICT   67 (Map on page 68)
  North Main Street 67, 1st Street 70, 3rd Street 72, 4th Avenue 76, 5th Avenue 78, Duck Pond Area 79, 6th Avenue 82, 8th Avenue 84, 10th Avenue 85, Gainesville Regional Airport 86

- V.   NORTHWEST DISTRICT   87 (Map on page 88)
  1st Street 87, 2nd Street 91, 4th Street 94, 5th Avenue 95, 6th Street 97

v

VI. WEST UNIVERSITY AVENUE and NORTHWEST 13TH STREET   100 (Map on page 101)
West University Avenue 100, 13th Street 111

VII. OUTLYING AREAS 112 (Map on page 113)

FURTHER READING   123

PART TWO: UNIVERSITY OF FLORIDA   129

A BRIEF HISTORY OF THE UNIVERSITY OF FLORIDA   131

I. AREA 1   134 (Map on page 135)
Century Tower 134, University Auditorium 136, Grinter Hall 138, Peabody Hall 139, Walker Hall 140, Carlton Auditorium 141, Little Hall 142, Tigert Hall 143, Criser Hall 144, Business Building 146, Bryan Hall 146, Matherly Hall 148, Anderson Hall 149, Smathers Library 150, Library West 152, Plaza of the Americas 152

II. AREA 2   154 (Map on page 155)
Turlington Hall 154, Griffin-Floyd Hall 156, Leigh Hall 157, Chemistry Laboratory Building 158, Flint Hall 158, Buckman Hall 160, Fletcher Hall 161, Sledd Hall 162, Thomas Hall 163, Murphree Hall 163, Academic Advising Center 166, Dauer Hall 166, Bryant Space Science Center 168, Newell Hall 169, Rolfs Hall 170

III. AREA 3   171 (Map on page 172)
Florida Gymnasium 171, Infirmary 173, Student Recreation and Fitness Center 173, Women's Gymnasium 175, Ben Hill Griffin Stadium 176, O'Connell Center 177, Van Fleet Hall 178, Perry Baseball Diamond 178, UAA Athletic Center 180, Beard Track and Field Complex 180, Linder Tennis Stadium and Ring Tennis Pavilion 182, College of Law 182, UF Golf Course and Bostick Club House 184

Contents

IV. AREA 4   186 (Map on page 187)
Fine Arts Complex 186, Architecture Building 186, Music Building 189, Marston Science Library/CIS 190, The Hub 191, Williamson Hall 192, Weimer Hall 194, Weil Hall 194, Nuclear Sciences Building 196, Mechanical Engineering and Materials Science Buildings 196, Reitz Union 198, Newins-Ziegler Hall 199, McCarty Hall 200, Dairy Science Building 201, Rawlings Hall 203, Broward Hall 203, Mallory-Reid-Yulee Halls 204, Norman Hall 205

V. AREA 5   207 (Map on page 208)
Gator Corner Dining Center 207, Tolbert Area Residence Halls 207, Apartment Residence Facility 210, 1995 Residence Facility 210, Graham-Hume-Simpson-Trusler Halls 212, Baby Gator Nursery and Child Enrichment Center 213, Lake Alice Area 214

VI. AREA 6   217 (Map on page 216)
Beaty Towers 217, Jennings Hall 218, WRUF-UFPD Building 218, Florida Museum of Natural History 220, Bartram Hall 222, Carr Hall 222, Rogers Hall 224, Phelps Lab 225, Psychology Building 225, Engineering Buildings 227, Health Science Center/Shands Hospital 228, College of Veterinary Medicine 229

VII. AREA 7   231 (Map on page 232)
Harn Museum of Art 231, Center for the Performing Arts 233, Southwest Recreation Center 234, Entomology and Nematology Building 236, Fifield Hall 236, Microbiology and Cell Science Building 237

VIII. HERE AND THERE   238 (Map on page 239)
President's Mansion 238, Fraternity and Sorority Houses 238, Student Family Housing Villages 241, Institutes of Black and Hispanic Culture 242, Parking Garages 244, P.K. Yonge School 245, Official Campus Corner Entrance 246

FURTHER READING   247

INDEX   249

INTRODUCTION

WHEN *Money* MAGAZINE NAMED GAINESVILLE IN 1995 THE best place to live in the United States, many residents were proud that the many attributes of Gainesville and Alachua Coutny were recognized, but at the same time apprehensive that an influx of newcomers would overwhelm the infrastructure and make the area less desirable.

Much of what the city and county offer is tied to their location: an hour and a half from the sea (the Atlantic Ocean on the east and the Gulf of Mexico on the west), far enough north in Florida that they experience some change of season, but far enough south in the United States that they bask in sunshine most of the year. Other advantages are the vibrant cultural life and the variety of outdoor activities available.

The following pages are divided into two parts: the first deals with the city and, to a lesser degree, the surrounding county; the second deals with the University of Florida. While the town and gown have often been separate in their respective histories, they have also been intricately bound together. As one has prospered, so has the other; as one has seen strife, so has the other.

The following pages describe Gainesville, Alachua County, and the University of Florida, not in exhausting detail, but in terms of what visitors and residents would probably want to know. We have chosen what we think are the major buildings and sites in the area. For more information about the city and county, we suggest John Ben Pickard's guide to Gainesville and Alachua County (see Further Reading). For reading more about the University of Florida, especially its history, Sam Proctor's book is an invaluable resource (see Further Reading).

Guide to the University of Florida and Gainesville

The two writers (Laurie, who wrote about UF, and McCarthy, who wrote about Gainesville) and the photographer (Hartigan) have spent a combined sixty-five years living and working in Gainesville and have come to know its many wonderful parts. We hope this book allows others to share in that knowledge.

We dedicate this book to Dr. John B. Pickard, professor of English and author of two books on the city and county; and Dr. Samuel Proctor, professor of history at the University of Florida and author of the school's history. Unless otherwise credited, the photographs were taken by Karelisa Hartigan.

PART ONE

Kevin M. McCarthy

SHORT HISTORY OF ALACHUA COUNTY

LONG BEFORE THE FIRST SPANISH EXPEDITION ARRIVED OFF THE Florida coast in 1513, various Native American tribes inhabited the peninsula. Among those that lived in what would become Alachua County were the Timucuans. Throughout the sixteenth and seventeenth centuries, explorers like Hernando de Soto passed through this area, subduing the tribes with ruthlessness and terror. Much later, Franciscan missionaries came here to set up missions to convert the Native Americans and teach them how to cultivate crops—with some success in both endeavors. By the 1650s, Spanish ranchers were able to establish the largest cattle ranch, Rancho de la Chua, in what is known today as Paynes Prairie.

In the early 1700s, the English and their Native American allies destroyed many of the Spanish settlements and missions in the area, effectively ending the Spanish presence for decades to come. After the English captured Cuba, the Spanish traded all of Florida for Cuba in 1763, and so began the twenty-year rule of the English in Florida. British explorer William Bartram traveled through the area in 1774, describing what he called "...the astonishing native wild scenes of landscape."

In 1783, England gave Florida back to Spain as part of the Treaty of Paris. That helped secure the freedom of the thirteen American colonies after the Revolutionary War.

For the next thirty-eight years, Spain had a difficult time controlling the vast territory that made up La Florida and could not prevent thousands of American settlers from moving south into the rich lands and uninhabited territory. In 1817, the Spanish Crown granted much of this land to a Spanish merchant, Don Fernando de la Maza Arredondo, in hopes that he

GAINESVILLE

Confederate veterans on the steps of the county courthouse.

Florida State Archives

would settle here. But finally, in 1821, Spain gave up and ceded Florida to the United States.

Three years later, Alachua County was established, taking its name from a Timucuan or Seminole-Creek word meaning "jug" and referring to a bowl that continually offers natural gifts. The "jug" refers to a large sinkhole on Paynes Prairie that filled up with the debris of logs and plants and then, when the debris was cleared or sucked into the ground, emptied to form a large prairie. Ongoing conflicts with the Native Americans, who had been living in the area long before the whites arrived, erupted in what is called the Second Seminole War (1835–42). When it finally ended after almost seven years of intense fighting, over 1400 whites had been killed, and the Seminoles had either been killed, deported, or forced to flee south to the Everglades.

When Florida became a state in 1845, more farmers and planters arrived in Alachua County and settled down with their families to work the more than forty-five thousand acres under cultivation. The population of the county tripled to over eight thousand residents in the 1850s, but the Civil War slowed down the county's development.

The second half of the nineteenth century saw a great influx of settlers, both white and black, into the area, attracted by the temperate climate and the many opportunities opening up for those willing to work hard. The rapid expansion of Florida's railroad systems in the 1880s, coupled with the development of the cotton, phosphate, and citrus industries, helped the county's population grow to over 32,000 by 1900.

When the University of Florida came to Gainesville in 1906, it ensured steady growth for the county. (For a brief history of the University of Florida, see pages 131-133.) Though the area grew and developed, it did not experience the explosive growth experienced by some coastal Florida cities, partly because of the decline of the cotton and phosphate industries before World War I. The county's population grew to 38,000 residents by

First Courthouse
Florida State Archives

GAINESVILLE

1940. After World War II, the influx of veterans, many of whom attended the University of Florida, and the gradual shift of more businesses to be close to the campus resulted in more and more developments to the west of the downtown core. The 1964 opening of I-75 to the west of the city also resulted in a westward expansion of the city, culminating in the building in 1978 of the huge Oaks Mall, north central Florida's largest shopping center.

The county population passed 100,000 in 1969, reached 200,000 in 1996, and should approach 250,000 by 2010. The county measures about nine hundred square miles, and the population density is about 222 people per square mile. That means that, if all the county residents were to stand an equal distance apart, each person would stand about a football field away from the next person.

Because of the forty thousand students at the University of Florida, the median age of Alachua County residents was between twenty-eight and twenty-nine in 1994, compared to a median age of between thirty-six and thirty-nine for the rest of Florida. This makes the county one of the youngest in the state.

The streets in Gainesville, like Alachua Avenue, have been lined with trees since the early days.
Florida State Archives

SHORT HISTORY OF GAINESVILLE

THE FIRST COUNTY SEAT OF ALACHUA COUNTY WAS NEW-nansville, near the present-day town of Alachua. After Florida became a state in 1845, farmers and ranchers from Alabama and Georgia settled in the rich lands of Alachua County. In 1853, David Levy Yulee built the cross-state Florida Railroad from Fernandina on the Atlantic Ocean to Cedar Key on the Gulf of Mexico. When the railroad bypassed Newnansville, local settlers voted to move their county seat closer to the line to take advantage of the railroad line to ship the locally grown agricultural products.

The town, which was officially established January 24, 1854, was named Gainesville after General Edmund Pendleton Gaines (1777–1849). General Gaines was a well-known, much admired military man who had served in the War of 1812. He had captured the traitor Aaron Burr and later fought in the Second Seminole War (1835–42).

The new town of Gainesville, which consisted of some 103 acres, was bounded by present-day Fifth Avenue on the north, Sweetwater Branch on the east, Second Place on the south, and Second Street on the west.

Apocryphal stories to the contrary, the town was never named Hogtown.

General Edmund Pendleton Gaines
Florida State Archives

7

GAINESVILLE

The latter was actually an Indian settlement situated on Hogtown Creek near today's Westside Park. While the town could have been called Hogtown because of a small trading post near David Yulee's Fernandina–Cedar Key railway, more far-sighted individuals chose to honor General Gaines in the new town's name.

Gainesville grew during the Civil War (1861–65), serving as a Confederate Commissary and a refuge for people fleeing federal occupation of coastal cities. Soldiers fought two battles in the downtown Gainesville streets in 1864, and federal troops occupied it after the war.

Despite the problems caused by the war, residents established their first school, the Gainesville Academy, and in 1866 joined it to Ocala's East Florida Seminary, the forerunner of the University of Florida. In the next year, the Freedman's Bureau established the town's first black school, the Union Academy.

Gainesville was incorporated on April 14, 1869. By 1882, the city had about 2,000 residents, fourteen cotton gins, many citrus and vegetable farms, and three railways servicing the area. When severe freezes in the 1890s hurt the citrus groves around Gainesville, phosphate and lumbering became more important. In 1885, the city replaced its wooden courthouse with a red brick building, and the downtown business and commercial area expanded.

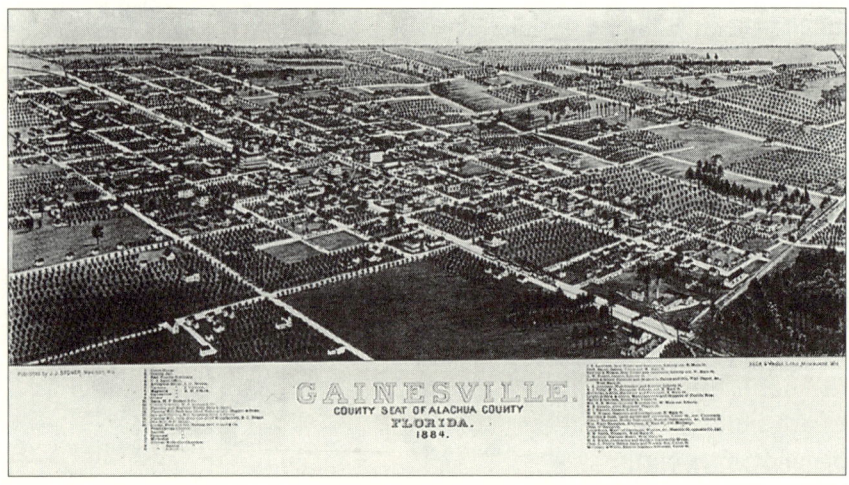

Gainesville in 1884

Florida State Archives

Short History of Gainesville

By the mid-1930s, when Gainesville and its suburbs had a population of about fourteen thousand, the University of Florida had just 2,500 students. The area then was a leading producer of tung oil, an oil obtained from the seeds of the tung tree and used for waterproofing and as a drying agent in paints and varnishes.

In 1996, the city had a population of about ninety-six thousand.

DOWNTOWN GAINESVILLE

Although much of Gainesville's expansion in the last few decades has been to the northwest, concerned citizens and developers have worked hard to keep the downtown area alive and prosperous.

The center of the downtown was a traditional gridiron pattern of eight blocks centered on a town square with the old wooden courthouse, which was built in 1856. Within four years of its founding, Gainesville's population was 269. Three hotels stood around Courthouse Square, in addition to several general stores. Within twenty years, several railways were servicing the town, and more and more stores and office buildings were built. When fires destroyed the wooden buildings in the 1850s, new, sturdier brick structures took their place. By 1890, the town's population reached 2,790, and ten years later totaled 3,633.

The establishment of the University of Florida in 1905 approximately twenty blocks west of Courthouse Square had a major impact on Gainesville's growth. The result was that Gainesville's corporate limits were increased in 1907 from 103 acres to five and a half square miles. This expansion led to the paving of West University Avenue to the university and the locating of many businesses along that road.

The downtown area struggled at times to keep its businesses, but was greatly helped in the 1970s by the building of a new city hall, courthouse, post office, and library. Downtown also acquired a plaza and outdoor amphitheater that have hosted community celebrations and have helped lead the way to new housing, for example, the elegant Arlington Square Apartments on Southeast Second Place.

Downtown Gainesville

The trains ran down the center of West Main Street.
Florida State Archives

Many of the older downtown stores and offices have been converted to restaurants, bistros, clubs, shops, and artists' studios. The Union Street Entertainment District along Southwest Second Avenue is a magnet for those seeking the ambiance of casual sidewalk cafe dining or late night music and dancing. New street signs combine the numbered street names with the older names (such as Union Street) that were dropped when Gainesville adopted the system of numbering its streets and avenues in the 1950s.

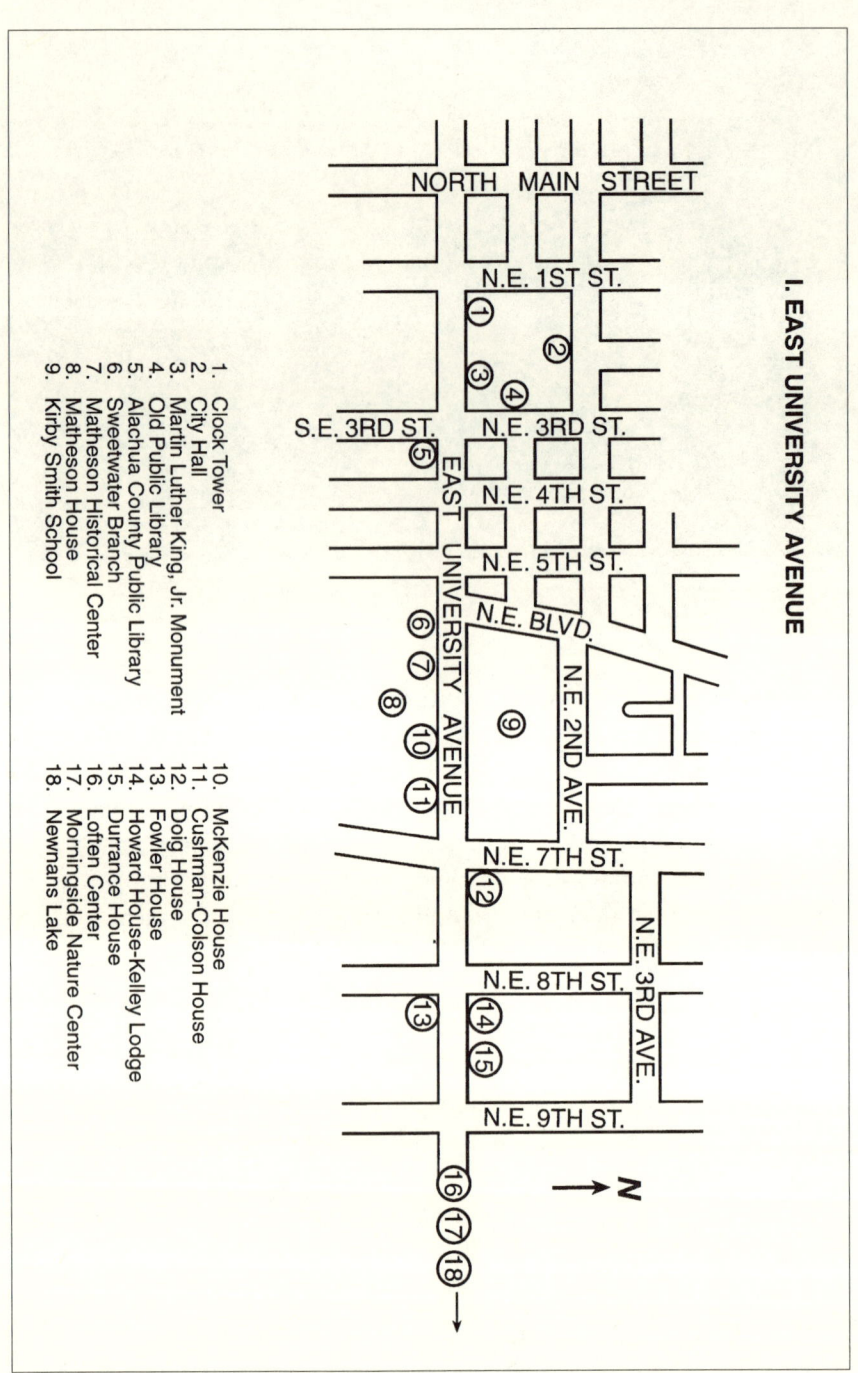

I. EAST UNIVERSITY AVENUE

1. Clock Tower
2. City Hall
3. Martin Luther King, Jr. Monument
4. Old Public Library
5. Alachua County Public Library Sweetwater Branch
6.
7. Matheson Historical Center
8. Matheson House
9. Kirby Smith School
10. McKenzie House
11. Cushman-Colson House
12. Doig House
13. Fowler House
14. Howard House-Kelley Lodge
15. Durrance House
16. Loften Center
17. Morningside Nature Center
18. Newnans Lake

I.
EAST UNIVERSITY AVENUE

1. Clock Tower
Northeast corner of East University Avenue and Northeast 1st Street

The handsome clock tower was completed in 1983, thanks to citizens' financial donations. The tower houses the old clock from Alachua County's second courthouse and borrows architectural features from the original 1885 courthouse. Because the original clock bell was joined with the city's fire-alarm system, many townspeople could hear its ringing and know when to be on the lookout for a fire. When workers tore down the old courthouse in 1961 to build the county's present building, the clock was stored away for several years and then moved to the grounds of the Florida State Museum on UF's campus, until a new tower was built for it in 1983. Ted Crom restored the clock to working order, and today it sits atop a forty-six-foot tower of brick and glass as a link with the city's past. On top of the clock tower, which is made of poured concrete and hand-molded brick, are a copper-plated roof, a weather vane, and a fence.

GAINESVILLE

2. **City Hall**
Across Northeast 1st Street from Trinity Episcopal Church

This modern building is a far cry from the quarters the city council and municipal court used to share with three horses and a volunteer fire department in the Number 1 Fire Station, located across from 116 Southeast 1st Street.

In the beginning of this century, the city rented offices at several sites, but officials eventually built a new city hall in 1927 at 117 Northeast 1st Street. The cost, at $98,950, was relatively high.

In 1935, in order to earn $200 a month and to attract a federal agency with its large payroll, the City Commission voted to rent out city hall to the Rural Resettlement Division of the federal government. Once again, city offices were placed in different locations in the downtown area for the next year and a half.

The original city hall was torn down in 1968 to make a parking lot for the new city hall nearby.

3. **The Martin Luther King Jr. Monument**
Southwest of the former library and in the Dr. Martin Luther King Jr. Memorial Garden

This monument by sculptor Buff Gordon (completed in 1988) honors the many African Americans in the area. It is inscribed with words from several of Dr. King's speeches.

East University Avenue

4. **Old Public Library**
On the northwest corner of Northeast 2nd Street

The new city hall annex once housed the county's main public library. The county library began in 1903, when the Twentieth Century Club, the forerunner of the Gainesville Woman's Club, was organized as a literary society and asked the public for donations of books and money. Soon after, it established a library. In 1906, the newly formed Library Association opened the Gainesville Public Library by combining the collections of the Twentieth Century Club, the East Florida Seminary (which later became part of the University of Florida), and a private library.

Between 1907 and 1912, the library had several locations. In 1918, with a $10,000 grant from the Carnegie Corporation, the Gainesville Public Library opened at 419 East University Avenue. In 1956, a new library was built at the site. By 1959, the library had branches in Hawthorne, High Springs, and Micanopy. Later, Bradford and Union counties joined the system, which was renamed the Santa Fe Regional Library. A new library was built in 1968 at 222 East University Avenue at a cost of $439,000; it could hold eighty-eight thousand volumes. In 1987, voters approved a $19 million bond issue to fund a new building on the site of the 1918 and 1956 buildings, and the construction of four new branch libraries.

New city hall annex, once the county's main public library.

5. **Alachua County Public Library**
   401 East University Avenue

Across the street from the old library is the county's new main library, built in 1991 at a cost of over $11 million. The three and a half acres that the library stands on were once the site of the original (1918) library building. The new 78,500-square-foot building, more than four times the size of the building it replaced, has a tall octagonal tower that lets in light to give the building a sense of openness. It holds 200,000 volumes and has meeting rooms available to the public. The staff at this headquarters library has increased from eighty to one hundred.

The building of this library across from the older library helped stabilize the downtown, a part of Gainesville that had seen a steady decline in the number of stores and businesses. Much of this decline was brought on by the coming of the automobile after World War II. In a community that prides itself on its educational institutions, the new library seems a fitting impetus to the revival of the downtown area.

6. **Sweetwater Branch**

This stream marked the beginning of Liberty Street, which became University Boulevard about 1905 (around the time that the University of Florida was established) and later, University Avenue. Live oaks along the avenue gave it a stateliness, a condition that is returning with the replanting of oaks in recent years.

7. **Matheson Historical Center**
   513 East University Avenue

The Alachua County Museum and Archives are housed in the restored American Legion Building, which replaced an auditorium known as The Tabernacle that the City of Gainesville owned. American Legion Post Number 16, which was organized in 1919 and named after Haisley Lynch, one of fifteen Gainesville men killed in World War I, laid the cornerstone for its new building here on Armistice Day, November 11, 1932.

The Matheson Historical Center, Inc., bought the building and renovated it in 1992. Today, this handsome red brick building has both permanent and traveling exhibits, a history research room, dioramas of the history of the area, and over two thousand books. It also holds extensive file

East University Avenue

Alachua County Public Library

Sweetwater Branch

GAINESVILLE

Matheson Historical Center

Matheson House

clippings on Alachua County history, as well as collections of eighteen thousand Florida postcards, twelve hundred "Stereo-View" cards, four hundred Florida prints, and many historical maps. Hours: Tuesday–Friday, 9 A.M.–1 P.M.; Sunday 1 P.M.–5 P.M. Phone: (352) 378-2280.

8. Matheson House
523 Southeast 1st Avenue (National Register, 1973)

Behind the Matheson Historical Center and on Southeast 1st Avenue is one of the oldest houses in Alachua County, and the second oldest in Gainesville, the Matheson House. Built around 1857 by Alexander Matheson, the house was later the home of Reverend Christopher Matheson, who served as mayor of Gainesville (1910–18) and a member of the Florida legislature (1917). The house has six free-standing wooden columns, four brick chimneys, a gambrel roof with three dormers, and cypress shingles cut in decorative designs. Christopher Matheson's wife, the late Sarah Hamilton Matheson, donated the house to the Matheson Historical Center for eventual use as a museum.

9. Kirby Smith School
620 East University Avenue

During the 1890s, when Gainesville became an important phosphate-producing center to replace the citrus industry that severe freezes had destroyed, the center of the city was the present-day Northeast section. The town's first public school, at University Avenue and Southwest 4th Street, then served the white student population in the late 1800s. In 1900, the city built a twelve-classroom, two-story brick school, called the Gainesville Graded and High School, on East University Avenue at the city's highest elevation. Officials later enlarged the school (1912) and renamed it Eastside Elementary (1923). In 1939, the two buildings were remodeled and renamed to honor St. Augustine-born Confederate General Edmund Kirby Smith (1824–93). General Smith was one of the last Confederate generals to surrender, and later became the president of the University of Nashville. He is one of two Floridians whose statue is in Statuary Hall, Washington, D.C.

Three of the first four principals of this school later became state superintendents of public instruction for Florida. One of the state's oldest pub-

GAINESVILLE

Kirby Smith School

lic schools became the main offices of the Alachua County School Board in the early 1980s. Today, school groups visit a restored old-fashioned classroom to learn about Gainesville history and re-create the "good old days."

10. McKenzie House
617 East University Avenue

This large house took its name from Reed McKenzie, who owned a motor company. The beautiful Victorian home was built in 1895 on what was then known as Alachua Avenue and became an office building in 1979. The house has had owners who were interrelated by marriage, including the McKenzie, Colson, Baker, Phifer, and Pound families.

The house is known for its three-story octagonal turret on the west side and the wraparound veranda that leads to an octagonal gazebo. The large size of the house reflects the city's prosperity during the 1890s. The house has fireplaces throughout, including the "widow's watch" room of the third-floor turret. The six-bedroom, five-bath home is best known for its wide front porch, as well as a European-style courtyard in back. The lot extends all the way to Southeast 1st Avenue and has a winding rear drive lined with flowers.

East University Avenue

11. Cushman-Colson House
625 East University Avenue

This house, built in 1885 on what was then called Alachua Avenue, suffered two bad fires before preservationists restored it to its original splendor. Built by Alonzo Cushman of Massachusetts, it served as his family's home for twenty years. During his career, Cushman worked as a cashier at the Dutton Bank, an insurance agent, a deputy clerk for the U.S. Court, the manager of the Hill Printing Company, a city councilman, and the Gainesville fire chief. His family sold the home in 1905 to Dr. James Colson, who served as president of the Alachua Medical Society. Colson was also a city councilman, a member of the Florida Senate, and in 1929 superintendent of the Florida Farm Colony in Gainesville, later known as Sunland and now called Tacachale. The next family to own the home operated it as the Alvarez Tourist Home for forty-five years. In 1992, it became the Sweetwater Branch Inn, the first bed-and-breakfast on University Avenue.

GAINESVILLE

12. Doig House
708 East University Avenue

James Doig, a prominent foundry owner and designer of industrial engines and machines, built this Italianate-style home in 1882. Doig's story was one of the many success stories of Alachua County. Having emigrated with his parents from Scotland to South Carolina when he was three years old, he later built an engine that was so small it could fit on a dime. The typesetting machine he invented alarmed the Charleston printers, who thought it would put them out of work and forced him to leave town. He then came to Florida in the 1850s on foot with all his belongings in a sack.

He worked hard and, in 1859, established the Doig Foundry and Machine Works in Gainesville. He served on the Confederate side during the Civil War, seeing action at the Battle of Gainesville on February 15, 1864. In 1867, voters elected him city alderman, and he, with eight other men, helped decide on Gainesville's name, corporate seal, and boundaries two years later. He invented an effective cotton gin that the local Dutton cotton-processing plant used and which was exported to Central America. He was also the first person in Florida to build a complete locomotive.

After Mr. and Mrs. Doig died in 1923, the building became a boarding house and eventually a single-family residence. In 1978, Jean and Terry Marshall bought it and remodeled it into an ophthalmologist's office. Noteworthy are the two identical porches on either side of the projecting front parlor. One of the most unusual features of the interior is a trompe l'oeil mural on the parlor ceiling.

22

13. Fowler House
805 East University Avenue

This Queen Anne Victorian house was built around 1906 by James Fowler, whose family lived in the house until the late 1960s. Before Fowler bought this house, the property had been owned by some of Gainesville's most prominent families, including those of J.B. Bailey (one of the city's early settlers), James Doig (the owner of the area's main foundry and machine works), T.F. King (Judge of the Circuit Court in the 1890s), and B.R. Colson (owner of the Alachua County Abstract Company).

Mr. Fowler was an important business person at the turn of this century, working as a real estate broker and owner of the city's first Buick agency and the city's first gas station (the "Just Right" station). He also served as steward in the Methodist Church, a member of the local Chamber of Commerce, one-term member of the Board of County Commissioners, two-term member of the City Council, and two-term mayor (1925–26).

The house features steeply pitched roofs, a mixture of exterior wood frame and shingles, and a round tower that rises to the third story from a circular gazebo on the western corner of the porch. The three brick chimneys served six interior fireplaces and the kitchen cooking stove. The balconies, bay windows, and gables give the distinctive house a look of projecting outward, and the ionic capitals that decorate the circular columns of the porch give the whole structure a stateliness.

14. Howard House–Kelley Lodge
810 East University Avenue

Originally built in 1883 as the winter home of Pittsburgh glass manufacturer Andrew Howard, this building was remodeled and enlarged as a boarding house known as The Lodge (1923–25). Howard also served as president of the Alachua Steam Navigation and Canal Company, which operated steamers to haul freight across Paynes Prairie, which was a lake in the 1870s. Mr. Howard and his family spent their winters here and, in the early 1900s, decided to live in Gainesville permanently. Mr. Howard died in 1904, before he could permanently move into the house, but his widow lived here until 1925.

At that time, McKee Kelley of St. Petersburg, Florida, bought the house and converted it into a boarding house. Kelley is best known for building the Dixie Hotel, a tall structure on West University Avenue that later became the Seagle Building. When the Depression wiped out Kelley's fortune, the Howard heirs took over the Kelley Lodge and ran it as a boarding house, "The Lodge," in the 1930s. In 1941, Ben Crawford bought the property and renamed it the Crawford Tourist Lodge. The Salvation Army bought it in 1969 and used it for its local headquarters. In 1987, Mary and Mark Barrow restored the house and converted it into medical offices, winning an award for outstanding adaptive reuse of a historic structure. The landscaping includes native Florida plants and herbs, each identified with a marker.

15. Durrance House
824 East University Avenue

This two-story, post-Victorian structure, which was built around 1914, takes its name from Oscar and Mattie Durrance, who owned the home from 1946 to 1982. Mr. Durrance was the founder of First Federal Savings and Loan, and assistant U.S. Postmaster. Attorney Eilon Krugman-Kadi bought the home in 1982 and, after doing much to restore it to its original condition, converted it into a law office. The maple flooring and placement of several distinctive antique pieces give the house a special flavor. This office is typical of the many buildings that doctors and attorneys have renovated for professional use, a practice that has aided in the stabilization of the downtown area. One of the big advantages of such buildings is that they are zoned for commercial use, unlike many of the older areas.

GAINESVILLE

As noted earlier, East University Avenue east of Sweetwater Branch used to be called Alachua Avenue. Originally, it was a tree-lined boulevard with large Victorian houses on both sides. The area to the Avenue's east has been restored in recent years to its former splendor. Professional offices and stylish residences between Northeast 6th and 9th Streets contain tourist homes and the Salvation Army. Mary Barrow and her doctor husband, Mark, who worked hard to preserve Alachua County's past, have restored many of these buildings.

16. **W. Travis Loften Center**
3000 East University Avenue

The Loften Center land was originally bought by the federal government to build a veterans' hospital. When officials decided to build the hospital on Archer Road, the federal government gave the land on East University Avenue to the Alachua County school system, which built a school there and established a vocational program. When the programs grew into an agribusiness center and became a high school, officials named it the W. Travis Loften Educational Center to honor W. Travis Loften, an educator who spent over forty-four years (1931–75) teaching and working in Florida's educational system. Today, the Loften Center offers classes for high school credit as well as classes in acquiring job skills, for example, in building construction, auto mechanics, and machinery. The Center also offers several dropout prevention programs for high school students and another program designed to encourage young people to return to school. A child-care center and parenting classes are available to the Center's students, all of whom have chosen to attend classes there.

17. **Morningside Nature Center**
3540 East University Avenue

About three miles east of downtown Gainesville is a Living History Farm. The farm includes an 1840 cabin and barnyard animals, and the Half Moon Schoolhouse, as well as seven miles of trails and boardwalks that take walkers through 278 acres of woodland containing many kinds of birds, mammals, and reptiles. This wildlife sanctuary and environmental education

East University Avenue

W. Travis Loften Center

Half Moon School at Morningside Nature Center

center attracts more than twenty thousand visitors a year, as it transports twentieth-century visitors back a hundred years. The park is meant to show visitors what north Florida was like before European settlement, as well as how pioneer Floridians were self-sufficient in growing crops and living off the land. Open 9 A.M.–5 P.M. daily. Children and adults may take part in farm chores daily at 4 P.M. Free. Phone: (352) 334-2170.

18. Newnans Lake

The 7,400-acre lake to the east of town is a popular site for boating and fishing. Located at the eastern end of East University Avenue and north of the Hawthorne Road (State Road 20), the kidney-shaped lake is the largest body of water in the area. Most of the lake is surrounded by a marshy area with many flooded cypress trees that provide a rich haven for bass. A boat dock and park south of town and just west of a popular fishing camp on the Hawthorne Road is a popular picnic area.

When Native Americans lived around the lake long before white settlers came here, the name of the lake was Pithlachoco. The white settlers renamed it to honor Colonel Daniel Newnan, an officer of the Georgia militia. Today, anglers from around the country fish for speckled perch and large-mouth bass in the lake, and ornithologists look for bald eagles, ospreys, and wood storks in the nearby woods.

The boat dock on Newnans Lake

II.
SOUTHEAST DISTRICT

THE DEVELOPMENT OF GAINESVILLE IN THE MID-1880S WAS primarily to the north of Courthouse Square because the original town plat had thirty-eight blocks to the north and only fourteen to the south. Southeast Gainesville was mostly a citrus grove in the 1800s, but that changed when severe freezes destroyed the local citrus industry and businessmen began building residences in the area.

The section of Gainesville bounded by East University Avenue, Southeast 9th Street, Southeast 5th Avenue, and the Sweetwater Branch is known as the Southeast Historic District. This area, which was developed between the 1880s and the 1920s, was listed on the National Register of Historic Places in 1988. Toward the end of the nineteenth century, Gainesville expanded in several directions, including the southeast. Here there were many orange groves, but it became more of a residential area in the 1890s.

Many of the merchants, leaders in local business and industry, built the large Victorian houses in this section. Gainesville, the fifth largest city in Florida by the end of the nineteenth century, was thriving because of its cotton, phosphate, and railroad business. After World War II, many of the large homes were converted into rooming houses or multiple-family residences. In the 1980s, scores of these houses were restored, and some were made into offices and bed-and-breakfasts, which has preserved the unique character of the area.

As one can see from the street signs that have both the old name and the new number, especially in the downtown area, the streets used to have names. Southeast 1st Avenue, for example, was once East Union Street, and Southwest 1st Avenue used to be West Union Street.

II. SOUTHEAST DISTRICT

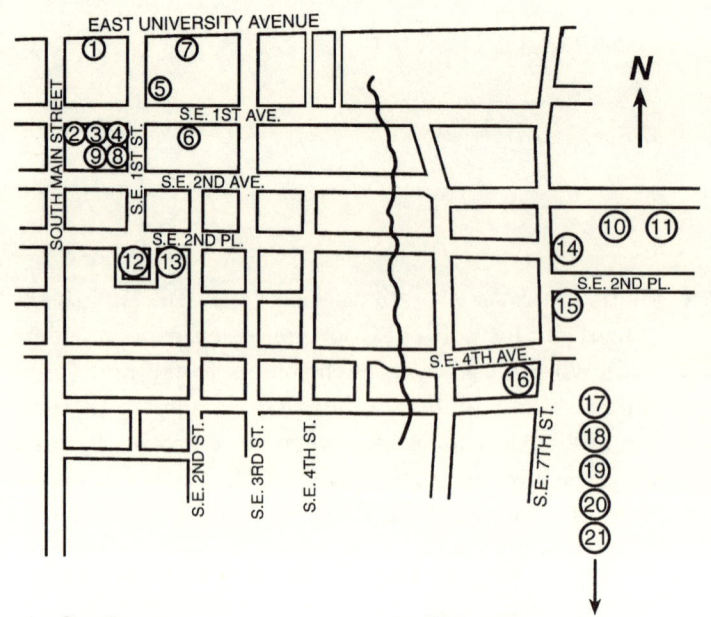

1. Courthouse
2. Scruggs, Carmichael Building
3. Barnes Building
4. Baird Theater-Cox Building
5. Bethel Gas Station
6. Star Garage
7. Community Plaza
8. New Baird Building
9. Sovereign Restaurant
10. Hodges House
11. Fagan House
12. Hippodrome State Theatre
13. Sun Center
14. Swearingen-Austin House
15. Baird House-Magnolia Plantation
16. Gray House
17. Joseph Williams Elementary School
18. Lincoln Middle School
19. Shopping Center
20. Boulware Springs Waterworks
21. Evergreen Cemetery

Southeast 1st Avenue

1. Courthouse

Newnansville, located in the northwestern part of the county, had served as the county seat since the incorporation of Alachua County in 1824. When the citizens of Alachua County met at Boulware Springs in 1854 to choose a new county seat, they wanted one that would be close to the proposed Fernandina–Cedar Key Railroad. One wealthy landowner, William Lewis, suggested the new town be called "Lewisville" after himself. Others wanted to name it "Gainesville" after Seminole Indian War hero Edmund P. Gaines. The moderator, Major James Bailey, proposed a compromise: If the citizens voted to build a new courthouse in the new town, they could call the town "Gainesville"; if not, the town would be "Lewisville." Lewis agreed, confident that the people would not be willing to pay for a new courthouse. But when a local building contractor, Tilman Ingram, offered to construct the new building for only $5,500, they accepted his offer, and the town became Gainesville.

The men who actually built the town's first wooden courthouse in 1856 were W.L. and Mike Finger. That first building had four offices on the first floor, and a courtroom on the second floor with a small room off to the side for jury deliberations. Several attorneys also had offices in the courthouse. Slowly, other buildings went up around Courthouse Square, which became the center of both the town and the county. The town's first street lamps were erected on the square in 1877. In 1915, the lamps were electrified.

That first courthouse had problems: The courtroom could not be heated, and wet weather tended to cause mold on the court records. In 1883, while drilling an artesian well for water, workers discovered gold 173 feet below the courthouse square. Sadly, they found it would cost more money to extract the gold than it was worth.

In 1885, a new courthouse with a flying eagle above a clock tower replaced the older structure at a cost of $50,000. The new building had four entrances to appease the store owners in each direction. It also had magnificent doors and the state seal inset near the roof line.

GAINESVILLE

Old Alachua County Courthouse
Florida State Archives

In 1904, the Kirby Smith Chapter (#202) of the United Daughters of the Confederacy installed on the northwest corner of Courthouse Square the statue of the Confederate soldier that is still there. The dedication reads, "In memory of the Confederate dead, 1861–65." The two other inscriptions read, "They counted the cost and in defence of right they paid the martyr's price" and "They fell for us, and for them should fall the tears of a nation's grief."

Between 1905 and 1908, the courthouse was remodeled. A weathervane replaced the eagle, and a bandstand was added. In 1958, a new unit just north of the courthouse replaced the older building, which was then torn down. The new building, called the Alachua County Administration Building, was dedicated in 1962. In 1978, a new courthouse, the Judicial Center east of the old courthouse, replaced the third one at a cost of $4.6 million. The new building was built east of Southeast 1st Street, which became the Downtown Plaza.

Southeast District

New Alachua County Courthouse

Scruggs, Carmichael Building

2. **Scruggs, Carmichael Building**
1 Southeast 1st Avenue

This two-story, brick commercial building was first called the "Porter Building" after its first owner in the 1880s, land attorney Watson Porter. For most of the time from 1902 to the 1970s, the west side of the first floor was occupied by the H.M. Chitty & Co. men's clothing store. The east side of the first floor was a dry-goods store (1903), a bowling alley (1905), a restaurant (1908–15), a millinery store (1922–28), and for many years, Fold's Hardware Store. For a while, the building was owned by Joseph Haymans, the largest single owner of timberland in Florida and the president of Gainesville's Florida National Bank. Today, the law firm of Scruggs and Carmichael occupies the building.

3. **Barnes Building**
7, 9, 11 Southeast 1st Avenue

This building, which dates from around 1887, is named after the man who built it, Louis Barnes, a land attorney and registrar of the United States Land Office in the late nineteenth century. In the first quarter of this century, grocers, barbers, and clothing dealers had stores in the building. More recently, the building has been the site of a department store (late 1920s), variety store (late 1930s–70s), beauty salon (late 1930s–1970s), and a restaurant (1990s).

4. **Opera House-Baird Theater-Cox Building**
19 Southeast 1st Avenue

This was originally called the Edwards Opera House (1887) after its builder, J.F. Edwards. The structure had seven stores on the first floor, five facing the public square in front and two facing Southeast 1st Street. On the second floor, over the two stores on the west, there was a photographer's studio, while an opera house used the space above the three stores on the east. When Eberle Baird bought the building in 1906, he added one and a half stories to the opera house part, built a balcony, and increased the seating to one thousand. The Baird Theater had stage, opera, and music productions for the town and the university through the early 1920s. It fared badly when motion pictures made their debut, and even worse when the university built University Auditorium (1925) on campus. In 1925, it

Opera House-Baird Theater-Cox Building

became a movie theater, but closed when Florida Theatre opened on West University Avenue in 1928. After a 1938 fire destroyed the Cox Furniture Store on South Main Street, it became an expanded Cox's Furniture Store and then was restored and repainted to become, in 1993–94, a restaurant and offices.

5. **Bethel Gas Station**
Corner of Southeast 1st Avenue and 1st Street

This Renaissance-Revival–style structure, built around 1925 and one of the few relatively unaltered service stations from the 1920s, was at first red brick, then was painted white in the 1930s. Preservationists saved it from demolition in 1976, and in 1987, when the downtown area was being renovated, moved it from its original site to its present location and restored it to its original look. It takes its name from Bethel Honeycutt, who took over the station in 1972. Two years later, the city obtained the property through eminent domain with the intention of building a civic center on the site, but voters defeated that proposal. It now serves as a bus terminal for the Regional Transit System (RTS).

Bethel Gas Station

6. **Star Garage**
119 Southeast 1st Avenue

This block-long building has been called "the single most important transportation-related structure standing in the City of Gainesville" because it has been associated with horses, mules, cars, airplanes, and buses. Built in 1903, this building served as a place where one could buy and rent horses and mules which had been shipped in from Tennessee and Kentucky farms by train. The livery stable there also sold buggies and wagons in the early 1900s. Homeowners living in the area who did not have the room to stable their own horses could rent out stalls in this building. One can still see along the walls small windows which provided light to each horse stall inside.

In 1917, the building became the Star Garage, selling Cadillacs and Studebakers in one of the state's largest auto agencies. In the 1920s, a paint shop upstairs was used to paint airplanes. Then, after a fire in 1931, the building housed a Buick dealership, a bus station, and then another automobile dealership. Bus companies like Greyhound used the Star Garage as

Star Garage

their main terminal until 1939, when a new bus terminal was built west of the downtown area. As Gainesville grew and more and more people moved here, the automobile dealers who were downtown moved their shops to North Main Street, where many of them remain today.

In 1977, the city bought the masonry building of the Star Garage and renovated it, retaining much of the original exterior and interior timber. Before it began to house the state attorney's office and law offices in 1986, local people used it for a flea market, community theater, even a boxing ring. One can still see the large front doors, through which horse-drawn buggies, Studebakers, and buses once passed. Today, the 16,000-square-foot office building is once again a vital part of the downtown business area. It was placed on the National Register of Historic Places in 1984.

Southeast 1st Street

7. Community Plaza
Southeast corner of East University Avenue and Southeast 1st Street

Officials built the Community Plaza in 1976 as a Bicentennial project, using $200,000 provided by individuals, clubs, and corporations. Since that time, the plaza has generated much debate as to its merits. The bricks, for example, which came from buildings that used to be on the site, were very hot in the summer. The original plaza walls were too high for security purposes, and the lighting and irrigation fixtures were considered inadequate. However, since its remodeling in the 1990s, it has often been the center of public celebrations and events. Besides bricks, the Plaza has other material recycled from old Gainesville. For example, the dirt in the planters came from the old baseball field at Harris Field on Northeast 8th Avenue and Waldo Road.

Southeast District

8. **New Baird Building**
112–116 Southeast 1st Street

Southeast 1st Street once had trees along each side. In the late 1800s, these trees provided shade and a place for riders to tie their animals. At that time, the City of Gainesville passed ordinances forbidding people from riding their horses across the wooden sidewalks and into the downtown stores. The New Baird Building, built in 1911 by Eberle Baird, the man who established Baird Hardware, has housed a candy store, automobile showrooms, a furniture company, and Mike's Bookstore and Tobacco Shop. For many years, Lillian's Music Store, a popular bar at the site, has leased part of the first floor. The second floor, which can be reached by a central staircase from the street, serves as offices and has skylights that provide lighting and ventilation for the perimeter offices. In the 1920s, the first floor on the north was joined to other buildings on the block as part of the Gainesville Chevrolet Sales Company, continuing a trend of having automobile showrooms in the downtown area. The building still retains its original detailing, interior pressed metal ceilings, and operable skylights.

Southeast 2nd Avenue

9. **Sovereign Restaurant**
12 Southeast 2nd Avenue

Originally a livery stable and carriage house for the Baird Theater (1910), then a parking garage when the coming of the horseless carriage made liveries unnecessary, this yellow brick building became a restaurant (1973) modeled after the Court of Two Sisters, a Creole restaurant in the French Quarter of New Orleans. Its arched carriage entry, below a raised center parapet and set between two arched openings, leads to the restaurant through an ornamental iron gate and covered alley. The restaurant, which has a brick-paved rear courtyard and solid exposed trusses, has been cited as a good example of adaptive reuse of a garage to a restaurant, allowing the owners to conserve the building.

In a college town that has more than its share of fast-food restaurants, this restaurant, often referred to simply as 12 East, has brought an elegance

GAINESVILLE

and old-city charm to the downtown. One story about the building when it was a livery stable told how a man, hiding on a porch across the street, shot his own brother full of buckshot for dancing with the first man's girlfriend the night before.

Sovereign Restaurant

Hodges House

10. Hodges House
715 Southeast 2nd Avenue

One of the most impressive restored homes in this district, the Hodges House was originally located near Holy Trinity Church in the downtown area, where it served for many years as the church's Sunday school offices. The house takes its name from its owner, Dr. James Hodges, a physician for the university and the president of the Florida Medical Association (then called the Florida Medical Society) in 1899. He also served as physician for the Seaboard Coast Line Railway and Atlantic Coast Line Railroad for more than three decades and ran a small, private hospital in town before the establishment of Alachua General Hospital. His medical degrees were from Johns Hopkins University, Harvard Medical School, the University of Heidelberg, and the University of Vienna.

This house in the Queen Anne Revival style was built in 1887. Hodges remodeled it, adding a wraparound porch and nine columns, a side turret, and a nearby two-story bay. Preservationists Mary and Mark Barrow saved the house from demolition in 1979, moved it to its present site, and converted it into four stylish apartments. The Victorian blue-gray color (the result of twenty mixes to obtain the right tone) with white trim add to the distinguished appearance of the 4,200-square-foot house, now called Victoria Square Apartments.

11. Fagan House
725 Southeast 2nd Avenue

This craftsman bungalow, which was built around 1910, had many owners, including the Fagans, owners of Fagan's Shoe Store downtown. Abandoned for five years and actually condemned by city officials before it was completely remodeled in 1982, the house features a dormer with three windows above the front door and a porch with three bay windows and four square columns. This 1800-square-foot house has been restored to what it originally looked like, although the addition of a modern kitchen, wooden deck to the back, and a tulip-design stained glass window in the back door have added charm and elegance to a building that was almost razed to make room for a new structure.

Southeast 2nd Place

12. Hippodrome State Theatre
25 Southeast 2nd Place

This impressive building in the Beaux Arts Classical architectural style was once the United States Post Office (1909–64) and later the Santa Fe Junior College (1966–67). While it served as the post office, officials used its second floor as a federal courtroom. Its six Corinthian columns at the front, bronze entry doors and terrazzo floors, beautiful carvings on the facade, and the concrete roof make this building one of the cornerstones of downtown Gainesville.

Begun in 1972 by five graduates of the University of Florida's Theater Department, the "Hipp" staged its first production in 1973 at a converted convenience store at 3401 Southwest Hawthorne Road. In 1976, the company moved to a warehouse at 1540 Northwest 53rd Avenue, but the noisy summer rains on the tin roof later convinced the troupe to move downtown. When the federal government built a new downtown post office in the 1960s, it transferred the old building to local power. After extensive renovations in 1980, it became the Hippodrome State Theatre, and in 1982 began offering top-quality dramatic productions. The Hippodrome is one of only four state theaters in Florida.

13. Sun Center
101 Southeast 2nd Place

This building originally housed the Pepper Publishing Center, and later the offices and printing press of *The Gainesville Sun*, the primary newspaper of the town. When the *Sun* moved to a new building on Southwest 13th Street in 1984, the buildings were renovated to become a mall with retail shops and restaurants that were meant to cater to the many visitors to the area as well as the hundreds of government and private-sector employees who work downtown.

The renovation of Sun Center was part of the city's $14 million project to redevelop downtown. Many businesses in the area were helped

The old post office/Hippodrome was the focal point of Southeast 1st Street in 1919 and remains so today.

Florida State Archives

when a parking garage was built south of the county courthouse to accommodate over four hundred cars. Another effort to make the area more aesthetic was the placing of electric wires underground. The elegant Arlington Square Apartments that Ken and Linda McGurn built nearby have also added much to the downtown area.

Southeast 7th Street

14. Swearingen-Austin House
205 Southeast 7th Street

Typical of the many fine houses in the Southeast District is this large Victorian house, built in 1903 by Thomas Swearingen, a lumber and turpentine businessman who also owned one of the city's first automobile

GAINESVILLE

Swearingen-Austin House

dealerships, the Swearingen Auto Company. Among subsequent owners of the house were George Dell (a Gainesville grocer and a member of one of the oldest families in the county), Hal Batey (a wholesale grocer, city commissioner, and a two-term mayor of Gainesville), and Henry Gray (longtime city attorney and Gainesville mayor).

In 1957, the house was bought by noted ornithologist Oliver Austin (author of *Birds of the World*) and his wife, Elizabeth Austin (author of *Frank M. Chapman in Florida*; Chapman was another ornithologist). For twenty-five years, Oliver Austin directed the Austin Ornithological Research Station at Wellfleet in Cape Cod, Massachusetts, which he and his father had founded in 1929. While Oliver was a curator of ornithology (1957–73) at what became the Florida Museum of Natural History, he increased the museum's collection of birds from 1800 to 17,500 catalogued specimens.

In 1978, the Barrows bought the house and converted it into apartments with balustrades and wraparound porches. Note especially the upper and downstairs porches.

15. Baird House–Magnolia Plantation
309 Southeast 7th Street

This three-story house, built in 1885–86, is one of Gainesville's most elegant (and its first) bed-and-breakfasts. The "rules" in effect set the tone: One, take your watch off at the door; two, eat when you are hungry; three, sleep when you are tired; and four, wake up whenever you feel like it. The building's long bay windows, tall Victorian tower, and ornate moldings are part of what makes this Gainesville's only extant example of the French second-empire style home. Most of its fifty-four windows go from floor to ceiling, and the 5,400-square-foot house has six guest bedrooms, each named for a different flower and having its own color scheme.

The house takes its name from Emmett Baird, who bought it in 1900, and it remained in his family until 1950. Emmett was president of Standard Crate Company and, along with his brother, Eberle, built Baird Hardware, a very successful wholesale hardware store in town that supplied many farmers and fruit growers in the region with thousands of baskets and vegetable crates.

The house was restored in 1991 and is now the elegant Magnolia Plantation Bed and Breakfast Inn. It takes its name from the trees that border the house. After 1950 and before it became a bed-and-breakfast, the house served as an alternative school (the Windsor School of Learning) and the home to a theater group. In the past few years, many visitors have stayed in the beautiful house with ten fireplaces and a mahogany bannister.

16. Gray House
408 Southeast 7th Street

Built in 1927, this house became the residence of Lucian Gray, a contractor who built the nearby Eastview subdivision in the 1920s. He also owned a rock quarry and trucking firm, and was the paving contractor for several Gainesville subdivisions. The 2,500-square-foot house is on a lot on which there was originally a building that served as L. M. Gray's office and a two-car garage.

Many of the houses in this section of the city have a feature rarely found in other parts of the city: Their roofs are covered with French tiles and often decorated with hip knobs.

Southeast 7th Avenue

17. Joseph Williams Elementary School
1245 Southeast 7th Avenue

This school, which opened in 1938, honors Joseph Williams, a civic-minded African American who had petitioned for such a school. It had 150 students in its first year, and had to be expanded several times to accommodate the increasing numbers of youngsters who wished to attend. The enrollment rose eventually to six hundred in 1960. Many of the students were the children of the black soldiers who had been stationed during World War II at Camp Blanding, twenty-five miles north of Gainesville, and who came to town on weekends. After the war, many of those soldiers moved to Gainesville to raise their families. Williams School was integrated in the early 1970s, when Gainesville integrated all its schools.

Southeast 12th Street

18. Lincoln Middle School
1001 Southeast 12th Street

Originally a high school for African Americans, Lincoln shut down in December 1969 when a federal judge ordered desegregation of the local schools. Many of Lincoln's students objected to the closing of the school, because they valued the family atmosphere at the school. After several years, it reopened as a vocational center and then as a middle school.

19. Shopping Center
South of Lincoln Middle School on Waldo Road

This shopping center, which opened in 1970, was created through the Alachua Volunteers Investment Corporation (Alavic). It was to be run by blacks for blacks as part of an effort to help black businessmen become more involved in the business world. The shopping center has included a barbershop, record center, TV appliance store, laundromat, and grocery store. However, the venture has not done well, perhaps because of the lack of local support.

Southeast 15th Street

20. Boulware Springs Waterworks
3400 Southeast 15th Street

As early as 1884, Gainesville officials looked into the problem of providing water for the growing settlement. Water was not only necessary for daily needs, but also to extinguish fires, since most of the buildings were wooden. Their first attempt was to drill an artesian well on the courthouse square, but they found only gold. Unfortunately, the gold was too deep to make it worthwhile to extract.

In 1898, local officials bought Boulware Springs (pronounced "Bo-Ware") for $2,500 and built the town's first waterworks at the site.

The pumping station built here in 1891 pumped out 300,000 gallons of pure water a day through water mains that were installed in the most populated parts of the city, which at that time had just 4,500 residents. This abundant water supply helped lure the University of Florida from Lake City to Gainesville in 1905. Local officials promised free water to the school, an offer that was later rescinded when the university began to grow rapidly.

Southeast District

When water demands of the growing city outgrew the supply at Boulware Springs, city officials turned to the deep wells that are still used today. In 1913, a new facility, closer to the city, combined waterworks and an electric generating plant. The pumphouse at Boulware Springs continued to augment the city's supply until 1953. From 1953 to 1977, water from the Springs was used only for the Kelly Power Plant near Depot Avenue.

In 1996, the average Alachua County resident used about one hundred gallons of water each day. That meant that total water use was about twenty million gallons of water a day, which is about the same amount that flows over Niagara Falls every thirteen seconds.

When historians realized how important Boulware Springs was to the city's history, that the waterworks marked the transition of Gainesville from a small town to a modern city, they convinced local officials to clean up the site and make it into a park. The site of Boulware Springs, formerly on Kincaid Road (which was later renamed Southeast 15th Street), is on the National Register of Historic Places. It is also an American Waterworks Landmark.

The cold, clear water no longer flows into homes, but instead into nearby Paynes Prairie to help maintain its fragile ecosystem. In 1990, the city used the 110 acres of land that it owns at Boulware Springs to create a park with sports facilities and hiking/biking trails. Nearby is the rails-to-trails hiking/biking path that links Gainesville with Hawthorne seventeen miles away.

Southeast 21st Avenue

21. **Evergreen Cemetery**
On Southeast 21st Avenue between Southeast 4th Terrace and Southeast 5th Street

The fifty-acre, city-owned cemetery encompasses the "Old Cemetery," a four-acre section that contains the gravesites of the town's early pioneers. Among those pioneers are James Doig, inventor of a cotton gin who prospered here; Haisley Lynch, Gainesville's only World War I battle casualty and the Marine after whom the American Legion named its local post; the

Evergreen Cemetery

Mathesons: James Douglas, Alachua County treasurer; his wife, Augusta; and their son, Christopher, a seven-term mayor of the town; H.H. McCreary, publisher and editor of *The Gainesville Daily Sun* and a member of the Florida Senate; and Margaret "Maggie" Tebeau, founder of one of Gainesville's earliest schools.

In the southeast corner of the cemetery stands a monument to those members of the Gainesville Guards who died of yellow fever in 1888. The Guards, who had been sent to Fernandina, Florida, to keep order when a yellow fever epidemic broke out, brought the fever to Gainesville when they returned. The monument originally stood on the northeast corner of downtown Gainesville's Courthouse Square. In 1922, officials moved the monument to Evergreen Cemetery, and in 1996 it was restored and landscaped.

III.
SOUTH MAIN STREET AND SOUTHWEST DISTRICT

A's Gainesville grew in the twentieth century, the downtown area was the site of the courthouse, businesses, and hotels. To the south, several manufacturing companies were established along Main Street and Depot Avenue, which paralleled one of the railroads that served the town.

South Main Street in the 1890s had oxen and trains.

Florida State Archives

III. SOUTH MAIN STREET and SOUTHWEST DISTRICT

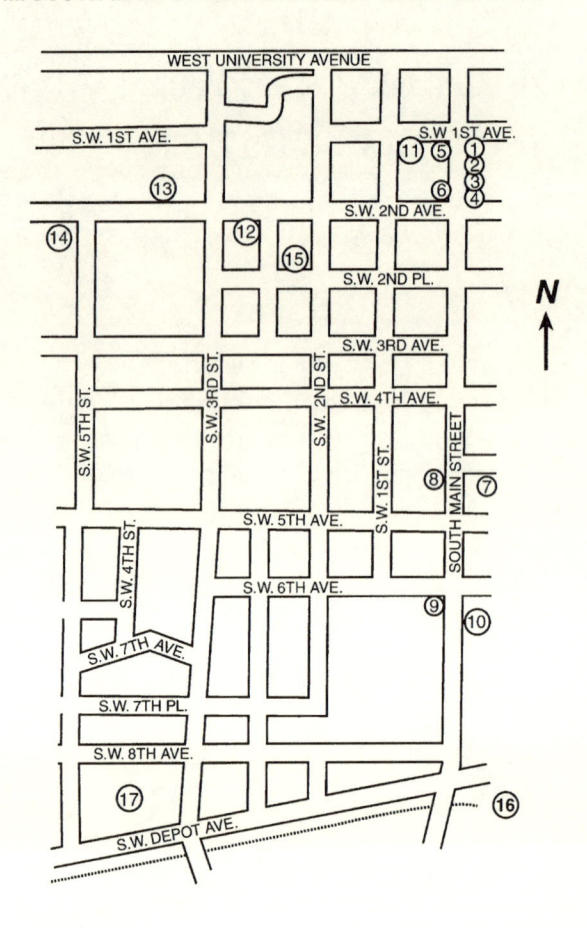

SOUTH MAIN STREET:
1. Porter-Haymans Woodbridge Building
2. Happy Hour Billiards
3. Office Building
4. Tench Building
5. Nightclub
6. Commercial Hotel
7. Fire Station No. 1
8. Lynch Park
9. Cox Furniture Company Warehouse
10. Baird Hardware Company Warehouse

S.W. 1ST AVENUE:
11. Rice Hardware

S.W. 2ND AVENUE:
12. Robb House
13. First Presbyterian Church
14. Alachua General Hospital

S.W. 2ND PLACE:
15. Jewish Synagogue

DEPOT AVENUE:
16. Depot
17. Porter's Quarters

52

South Main Street

1. Porter-Haymans-Woodbridge Building
109 South Main Street

This two-story brick building once housed the *Daily Sun* newspaper (early 1900s to 1926) and later the United States Tung Oil Laboratory (1930s and 1940s). Burtz Printing, which produced a city directory (1905–World War I), shared this building with the *Sun*, which moved in 1926 to its new facilities east of the old post office. H.H. McCreary published the newspaper from the late 1880s until 1917, when he sold it to the Pepper Printing Company. Over the years this building has housed an art studio, cafeteria, variety store, and beauty salon.

2. Happy Hour Billiards
111 South Main Street

In the 1890s, a two-story masonry barn and later, a furniture store and cabinet shop stood here. When the building was razed around 1912, a garage took its place and eventually became part of the Gainesville Chevrolet Company. When the car company moved out in the early 1930s, the garage was divided into two spaces, one of them for Melton Motors, Inc., and the other for Cypress Inn Billiards. The spaces were joined again in 1950 for Johnson Brothers, Inc., a feed store. In 1958, the building became Stud's Pool Hall, which was succeeded by Happy Hour Billiards.

3. Office Building
113 South Main Street

This single-story building, built in the late 1880s, was originally a meat market. It later served as a cigar factory, tin shop, tailor shop, welding shop, retail store, and a printing shop called The Wayside Press. From 1950 to 1958, it was Johnson Brothers, Inc., a feed store that also occupied the building to the north. More recently, 113 has served as professional office space owned, as is the Tench Building next door, by Chief Circuit Judge Benjamin Tench. In restoring this building, Judge Tench had a new frieze added several feet below the parapet with the dual purpose of adding style and catching pigeon droppings.

GAINESVILLE

Happy Hour Billiards

Tench Building

4. Tench Building
115 South Main Street

The two-story, brick building next door, with the words "Tench Building 1887" incised over the five arched windows at the second level, was the Samaritan Hotel in the 1890s. The hotel, which had a fireplace in each room, catered to the Savannah, Florida and Western Railroad that ran in front of the building. The building later became a plumber's office, a Chinese laundry, a gunsmith store, and professional offices. The Tenches became associated with the building when Judge Tench's uncle, Dr. J. Dawkins Tench, operated a dental surgery office on the second floor. Judge Tench opened his first law office in the building in 1949 after finishing law school at the University of Virginia.

5. Nightclub
104 South Main Street

At the beginning of this century, this building housed four small stores and a physician's office. The site was originally used by S.B. Duke's Saloon, a building that was razed and replaced by the present single-story building. University Furniture Company took over the building in the 1930s and made it into one store. This eventually became City Furniture, which stayed through the 1960s. In 1976, 104 became the Main Street Cocktail Lounge, a popular bar with its distinctive three iron posts at the corner entrance. It later became Richenbacher's, a popular night spot in the area that was named, with a little poetic respelling, after Eddie Rickenbacker, the World War I flying ace. The night spot closed in 1996 after eighteen years of operation. At the time, there were twenty-one nightclubs within a three-block radius, all competing for a similar crowd of college students and young professionals.

6. Commercial Hotel
120 South Main Street

This oldest existing hotel building in the city was built as the Alachua Hotel (1885). It changed names to White's Hotel (1892), Seminole Hotel (1910), Imperial Hotel (1920), and the Commercial Hotel (1924). It also housed the Hill Printing Company and the Pepper Printing Company (about 1900–20).

As a hotel, it took advantage of the fact that a railroad (the Savannah, Florida and Western) ran down the center of Main Street (then West Main Street) in front of the building. It closed as a hotel in the 1970s, but in 1983 was restored and renovated as a county office building.

The large street-level windows with semicircular transoms give the three-story building a distinctive appearance.

7. Fire Station No. 1
Between Southeast 4th Place and Southeast 5th Avenue

In the 1860s, one of the first acts of city officials was to establish a fire department committee. This led to the establishment of a part-time fire chief (at $40 a month) and a full-time assistant fire chief (at $60 a month). They were to oversee the thirty-five volunteers who manned the equipment. The volunteers were only paid when they fought a fire.

In the early days, the men had to drag their equipment to a fire, and could only hope that they reached it in time. After many requests, the city provided a horse for them. The horse was "on call" from the nearby Davis Livery Stable, located near the southeast corner of what is now Southwest 1st Street at 2nd Avenue. (This building was torn down to widen the avenue.) In 1890, the city bought a horse that could be used to haul fire equipment and also to carry the city trash. The horse was named "John" in honor of the first fire chief, John McArthur. By 1912, the department had three horses (John, Mack, and Arthur, all three named after John McArthur), which were traded in for one motor-driven fire truck. In 1925, the department became a full-time, paid operation under Chief E.F. Beville, who served from 1911 until 1952.

The old station across from 116 Southeast 1st Street, a site that the fire department shared with the city council and municipal court until a new city hall could be built in 1927, was torn down in the early 1960s to allow for the widening of 2nd Street.

In the early days, the fire fighters were on call even during their hours off. Each had an alarm at home that was connected to the station's alarm. The men would work twenty-four-hour shifts, with an hour off for meals and one day off a week. With the introduction of the aerial ladder around 1941, fire fighting improved dramatically.

When L.A. (Nick) Nicholoson became fire chief in 1958, he initiated several new programs to educate homeowners about potential fire hazards.

South Main Street and Southwest District

Commercial Hotel

Fire Station No. 1

8. Lynch Park
400 block on the west side of South Main Street

The 1.3-acre park, whose full name is Haisley Lynch Gardens, has a gray slab indicating that the park honors Haisley Lynch, the only son of Mary Helen and Louis Lynch. Haisley was killed on November 18, 1918, the day the armistice was signed at the end of World War I (see Evergreen Cemetery above). Mrs. Lynch, whose home once stood here, deeded the land to the city in 1956 for $10, with the stipulation that it always be a park.

9. Cox Furniture Company Warehouse
602 South Main Street

Resembling a Romanesque Revival church, this building (c. 1890) had a triple arched entrance and a side opening large enough for trains to enter for ease of loading. Abandoned after many years of use as a wholesale grocery warehouse and Cox Furniture Warehouse, the 17,000-square-foot building was remodeled into an office building in 1994. It is listed on the National Register of Historic Places.

Cox Furniture Company Warehouse

10. Baird Hardware Company Warehouse
619 South Main Street

This brick building (1910) used to be the main warehouse for Baird Hardware, one of the town's most important businesses for over ninety years. Today, several small businesses operate there, as well as the theater for the Acrosstown Repertory Players. Sometimes described as Gainesville's Off-Broadway, the eighty-seat theater produces experimental and avant-garde shows, as well as the classics. Phone: (352) 375-1321. The building has been listed in the National Register since 1985.

Southwest 1st Avenue

11. Rice Hardware
15 Southwest 1st Avenue

The long building at this site has seen many businesses since the early 1900s, including two furniture stores, two bicycle-repair shops, and a combination drugstore and physician's office. The furniture stores were Seagle Furniture Store, which remained here until 1936, and then University Furniture Store. The western part of the building was a grocery store in the 1920s and 1930s. Rice Hardware, which had been at 101 Southeast 1st Street since 1936, moved to this site in 1965 and eventually occupied the entire building. This single-story, yellow brick building evolved from the original five shops into a single retail space with wood columns. It has three pairs of beveled glass-entry doors set in the altered raked-brick facade.

Southwest 2nd Avenue

12. Robb House
235 Southwest 2nd Avenue

This one-story Victorian cottage was originally built on University Avenue (1878). In 1898, it became the medical office of Drs. Robert Robb and his wife, Sarah Robb, the town's first woman physician.

Robert Robb had come to Gainesville from Chicago, Illinois, to recover from tuberculosis, which he did. Because his wife, Sarah, had been refused admittance to medical schools in the United States, probably because she was a woman, she and her husband went to Germany, where she obtained her M.D. degree in Heidelberg after two years of study.

Robert and Sarah Robb came to Gainesville as one of the state's first husband-wife physician teams. They treated the sick and also operated one of the first private boarding schools in the county. After her husband died in 1903 at the age of 62, Dr. Sarah Robb continued to practice medicine out of the Robb House until 1917, specializing in the care of children and women and making her rounds in a horse and buggy. The Alachua County Medical Society eventually acquired the building and moved it to its present site. Robb House now houses a medical museum.

13. First Presbyterian Church
300 Southwest 2nd Avenue

The bell that calls the congregation to worship services today was used in 1864 to alert Gainesvillians to approaching Union troops. At that time, the church was situated on East Main Street one block north of the old post office.

The history of Presbyterians in Alachua County goes back to the original Kanapaha Church off Archer Road. A group of cotton farmers from South Carolina moved to the area in the 1850s and soon decided they wanted a church in which to worship. Around 1857, they convinced an Irish-born minister, Rev. William McCormick, to do mission work in the area. He then began a horse-riding circuit of towns that included Gainesville, Ocala, Micanopy, and Cedar Key. He founded churches in many towns, including Archer, Flemington, Micanopy, Orange Creek, and Wacahoota.

The Kanapaha church saw many of its members move to Gainesville as the town began to grow and prosper. In 1860, the congregation built on East Main Street a church that they shared with the Baptists, Episcopalians, and Methodists. The Presbyterians built their second church in 1867 and in 1953 moved to their present location. Other Presbyterian churches have since been built in the county to serve the needs of the people.

Among the Presbyterian church's ministers was Dr. Ulysses S. "Preacher" Gordon, who retired in 1968 after forty years of continuous service in the pastorate.

First Presbyterian Church

14. Alachua General Hospital
801 Southwest 2nd Avenue

Before the building of Alachua General Hospital in 1927, private hospitals, usually in large homes, served the health needs of the area. For example, Dr. William Buck's private hospital at 552 Northeast 2nd Avenue, the Williams Hospital at 405 Northeast 7th Street, and the Edwards Hospital on Southwest Depot Street were both infirmaries and private homes.

Alachua General Hospital, a full-service, not-for-profit health center, is located midway between the downtown area and the University of Florida. The over three hundred members of its medical staff represent over thirty specialties. When it merged in 1996 with Shands Hospital and AvMed Santa Fe, it began a new era. Officials now stress better service for patients rather than competing to fill beds. **Shands Hospital** (576 beds) at the University of Florida, **Alachua General Hospital** (423 beds), **North Florida Regional Medical Center** (267 beds), and the **Veterans Administration Medical Center** (349 beds) provide high-quality care to patients who travel here from around the country. Shands, for example, has the largest state-contained homecare operation and the sixth largest organ transplant center in the country.

Southwest 2nd Place

15. Jewish Synagogue
Corner of Southwest 2nd Place and 2nd Terrace

Two blocks west of Main Street, hidden by overgrown bushes and trees, is the site of the original synagogue built by the town's first Jewish families. The first Jewish family moved into Gainesville from Virginia in the late 1860s, after the Civil War. Moses Endel, the head of the family, had a store in what became the Woolworth Building on the northwest corner of today's University Avenue and Main Street.

Later, Jewish families established a cemetery on the corner of East University Avenue and Waldo Road, where the graves date back to the 1870s. The site, as is the Jewish custom, was outside the city limits. Among the gravesites is that of an entire family that died in the 1888 yellow fever epidemic.

In the 1920s a formal congregation was incorporated under state law as the Congregation B'Nai Israel (Brothers of Israel), and the synagogue was dedicated in 1924. The Jewish community also had a meeting place off Northwest 16th Avenue and 34th Street.

In 1938, the Hillel Foundation for University of Florida students was established and eventually moved into its present site at 16 Northwest 18th Street. The present Hillel building was built there in 1953. The B'Nai Israel Jewish Center was built at 3830 Northwest 16th Boulevard to serve the needs of the Jewish community.

Depot Avenue

16. Depot
203 East Depot Avenue

Depot Avenue is an east–west road named after the railroad depot that is just east of South Main Street. The depot is Gainesville's oldest train station. This building is also an excellent example of an early twentieth-century train depot that has kept its architectural integrity to a high degree. It was named to the National Register of Historic Places in 1996. The present building dates back to about 1907, but there were buildings on the site as early as the 1860s, when the Florida Railroad passed through here on the Fernandina–Cedar Key run.

The county seat was moved from Newnansville, which was several miles off the railroad route, to Gainesville in 1854 because of the location of the Florida Railroad. This made Gainesville a center of trade and commerce. The railroad's purpose was to help connect New York and New Orleans by providing a short land route between the port of Fernandina on the Atlantic Ocean and Cedar Key on the Gulf of Mexico.

The railroad, whose construction began in Fernandina in 1855, reached Gainesville in 1859 and Cedar Key in 1861 for a total of 155.5 miles.

At the outbreak of the Civil War in 1861, part of the railroad was dismantled. After the war, the Florida Railroad was succeeded by the Peninsular and West India Transit Company; still later (1872) by the Atlantic, Gulf and West India Transit Railroad; and (1884) by the Florida Railway and Navigation Company. When the Seaboard Coastline built a new passenger station on Northwest 6th Street in 1936, this old depot fell out of use. It served as a hardware store (1950–70s) and then as a storage warehouse.

17. Porter's Quarters

Just west of Main Street and north of Depot Avenue, Porter's Quarters is one of the oldest African-American communities in Gainesville. The area has two possible sources for its name. It may have been named for O.A. Porter, the man who developed the area in 1894 for black servants and laborers. Or it may have been named for Dr. Watson Porter, a white doctor from Canada who was principal of Union Academy and also mayor of Gainesville in 1873. He bought much land in the southwestern part of the city and sold it to African Americans to enable them to own their own land. He also encouraged newcomers to the black community to become self-sufficient farmers.

The area is bordered by Depot Avenue, Southwest 4th Avenue, South Main Street, and Southwest 6th Street. The area deteriorated until, in the late 1980s, the residents banded together and made improvements to the nearby park (Tumblin' Creek), where, around the turn of the century, the all-black "Central City Nine" baseball team once played their games. The residents secured a $2 million housing project called Porter's Oaks at Southwest 2nd Street and Southwest 6th Avenue. Dilapidated buildings were torn down and replaced with new dwellings that have brought pride to the area and helped drive away the criminal elements. The new homes enabled local citizens to own their own homes.

Residents also built Grandmother's Park on the corner of Southwest 5th Avenue and Southwest 4th Street as a safe place for youngsters to play. Also, the nonprofit Neighborhood Housing and Development Corporation has built new homes in the area and then sold them to people who would not ordinarily qualify for a mortgage. Finally, Porter's Community Center at Southwest 2nd Terrace and Southwest 6th Street gives neighborhood children a place to go to after school and on days off.

IV.
NORTH MAIN STREET AND NORTHEAST DISTRICT

North Main Street

This street, which used to be called West Main Street, was built over the Atlantic Coast Line railroad tracks.

1. **Bank Building**
104 North Main Street

Across the street, on a block that used to be owned by the Atlantic Coast Line (ACL) Railway and that was once the site of the main building of the train depot, there is a tall building that has served as a bank building and credit union. In 1948, the ACL decided to take up its tracks and switch its line to Northwest 6th Street, partly to avoid the forty-five-foot slope at the end of South Main Street. The slope was so steep that it took a lot of fuel to move the trains up to the top.

2. **Masonic Temple**
315 North Main Street

Built in 1908, this huge building is constructed in what is known as Beaux Arts Classicism style. It features a raised portico with large Doric columns at the front, and the Masonic sunburst designs are still visible on the large doors of the building. The Gainesville Lodge 41 was chartered by the Masons in 1857 or 1858.

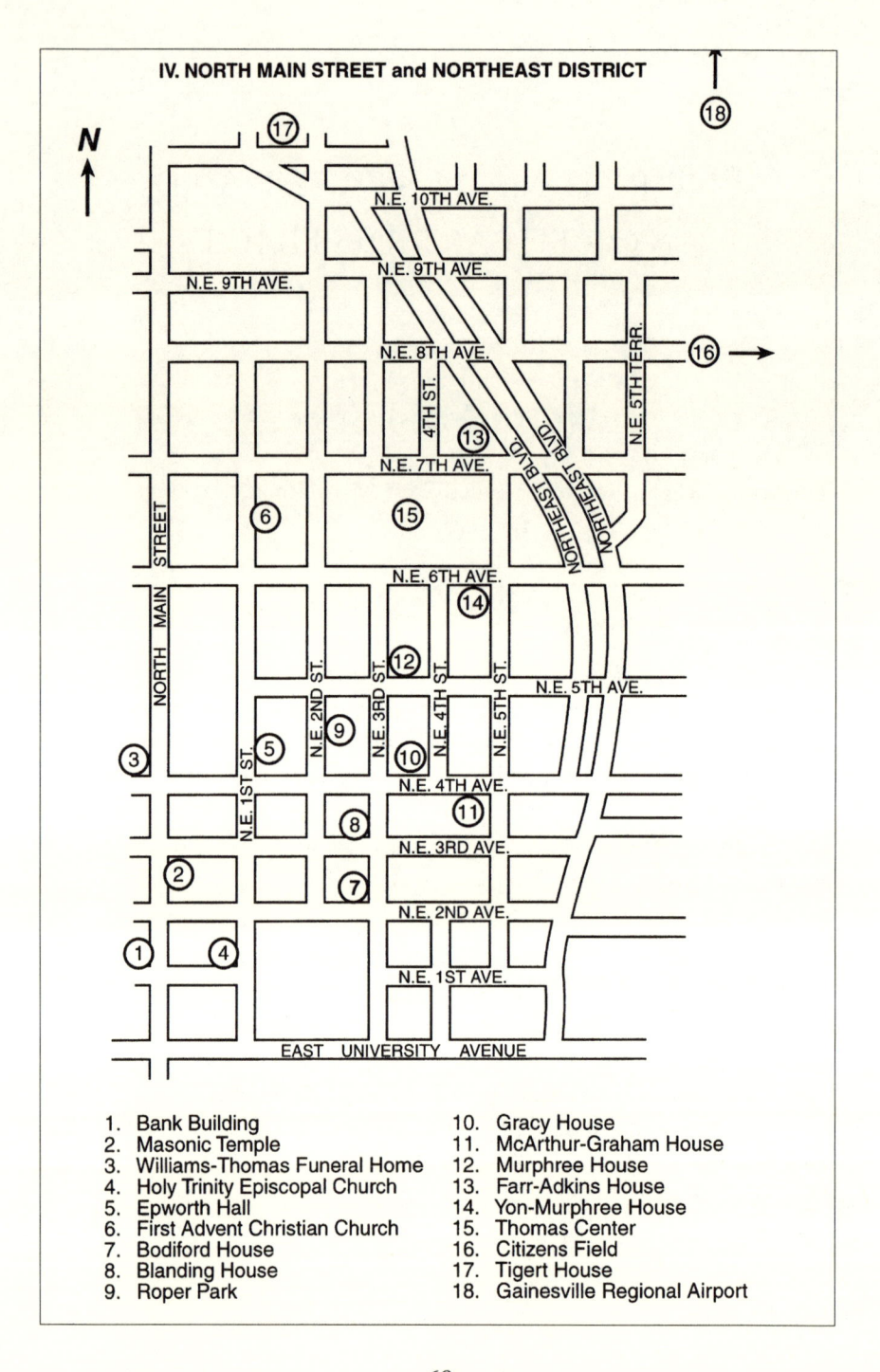

IV. NORTH MAIN STREET and NORTHEAST DISTRICT

1. Bank Building
2. Masonic Temple
3. Williams-Thomas Funeral Home
4. Holy Trinity Episcopal Church
5. Epworth Hall
6. First Advent Christian Church
7. Bodiford House
8. Blanding House
9. Roper Park
10. Gracy House
11. McArthur-Graham House
12. Murphree House
13. Farr-Adkins House
14. Yon-Murphree House
15. Thomas Center
16. Citizens Field
17. Tigert House
18. Gainesville Regional Airport

Masonic Temple

3. Williams-Thomas Funeral Home
404 North Main Street

With the old horse-drawn hearse housed in a glass display case outside, the Williams-Thomas Funeral Home represents one of the very few century-old, family-owned businesses in town. The other one is **Alachua County Abstract Company** (215 Southeast 2nd Avenue and 2632 Northwest 43rd Street). The funeral home was begun as a side business by Dr. Thomas Fraser Thomas, a medical doctor, in his downtown hardware store. (In those days, many hardware stores sold caskets and provided funeral services.)

In the past hundred years the business has twice been passed from father to son. The business became the Williams-Thomas Funeral Home when undertaker Dick Williams merged his business with the Thomases in 1954.

The office of the building on North Main Street was the old Thomas home. The family lived upstairs and conducted business on the first floor. The nineteenth-century funeral homes often had their own ambulances to provide yet another service to county residents.

Northeast 1st Street

This street used to be called East Main Street, even though it ran north–south, and paralleled West Main Street (now North Main Street). The Northeast Historic District preserves several important buildings from the early days of Gainesville. Many residences in this district retain a charm unique to the city, but others near North Main Street were razed to make way for banks and parking lots. Other homes on Northeast 1st Street going toward Northeast 8th Avenue were converted into offices. This downtown area attracts thousands of visitors to its annual arts festivals in the fall and spring.

4. Holy Trinity Episcopal Church
100 Northeast 1st Street

Only five families belonged to the Trinity Church in 1868, but the parish grew steadily. Five years later, they built a timber structure where the Masonic Temple stands today. In 1905, Bishop Edwin Weed laid the cornerstone of Holy Trinity Church at Mechanic and East Main streets, where the church stands today.

The first service was held in the incomplete church in 1907, when the congregation had about one hundred parishioners. After fire destroyed the church in 1991, parishioners rebuilt it at the same site, thus preserving a link with the church's history and with the many parishioners who had worshiped there. Among its notable stained glass windows is the Ascension Window. Fortunately, the window had been removed for repairs when the fire destroyed the rest of the church.

5. Epworth Hall
419 Northeast 1st Street

The East Florida Seminary, the predecessor of the University of Florida, began in Ocala, Florida, in 1852, and was funded by the state beginning in

North Main Street and Northeast District

Holy Trinity Episcopal Church

Epworth Hall

1853. The Seminary moved to Gainesville in 1866. At the time, the school had seventy-one students. When fire destroyed the original wooden classroom building in 1883, a new two-story brick building replaced it. This Renaissance-Revival–style building, which is now **Epworth Hall**, had four classrooms on the first floor and a study hall, library, and offices on the second floor. The building later became the White House Hotel when the present UF campus was established. In 1911, the First United Methodist Church bought the property and renamed it Epworth Hall after the English village where the founders of Methodism, John and Charles Wesley, were born.

6. **First Advent Christian Church**
617 Northeast 1st Street

One of the few remaining churches in the Northeast District, this Gothic Revival building was built in 1903 by a congregation that was organized in 1888 as the Second Advent Christian Church in Hague, Florida. This congregation should not be confused with the Seventh Day Adventist.

Northeast 3rd Street

The streets in Gainesville's quadrant system (Northwest, Northeast, Southwest, Southeast) used to have names instead of numbers. Thus, Second Avenue used to be Orange Street, and Third Avenue used to be Court Street.

7. **Bodiford House**
216 Northeast 3rd Street

An example of the many fine homes on this street is the two-and-half-story Bodiford, built in 1897–98 by Gainesville druggist James Bodiford and closely resembling the Richards House across the street to the east, which had been built by the same man. Bodiford had come to Gainesville in 1878, then worked in Cedar Key for twelve years as a druggist before returning to Gainesville, where he worked as a druggist until his death in 1934. In 1909, his peers elected him president of the Florida State Pharmaceutical Society. His daughter, Mary Jesse Bodiford, remembered the white picket fence around the yard and the nightly lamplighter who rode down the street at sunset to light the gas streetlights. Three generations of the Bodifords lived and died in the home before new owners allowed it to deteriorate.

Historic Gainesville, Inc. (HGI), a group of concerned citizens determined to preserve valuable structures from the past, bought the house in 1978 rather than see it destroyed and replaced by a parking lot. The organization bought the house, its first such purchase, because it considered it the cornerstone of the lower northeast historic neighborhood.

The Victorian-style house had eight bedrooms, each containing a fireplace. The ten-foot-high ceilings, large windows, and huge porch along the front of the house made the Bodiford a special place. After HGI renovated it, a group of UF architecture students rented it out and continued restoring it.

The Holbrook family restored it in 1981, making it into four apartments, but retaining the character and styling of the original house. One of the most unusual architectural features of the house is its diamond-patterned fish-scale siding on the second-floor balcony and part of the south side.

8. Blanding House
306 Northeast 3rd Street

Built in 1899 by Horatio Davis, a judge and two-time mayor of Gainesville, this Queen Anne–style house became the residence of Florida Guardsman Albert Blanding. Blanding lived in the house until 1922 and owned it until 1958. Blanding, a general in World War I and chief of the National Guard Bureau, may have been the only person to have a military installation named after him while he was still alive. Camp Blanding near Starke honors the general, who helped create the Everglades National Park after his retirement. General Blanding (1876–1970) is buried with his wife in Gainesville's Evergreen Cemetery.

In 1980, Jane and Gardiner Myers restored the house, making it into two apartments. Note the decorative shingles, scrolled trim at the gable ends, and turned spindles on the downstairs porch.

GAINESVILLE

Blanding House

9. Roper Park
The block bounded by Northeast 4th and 5th Avenues and Northeast 2nd and 3rd streets

Just behind Epworth Hall is the Parade Grounds where the students attending the East Florida Seminary once marched. At the north end of the park is the site of a large wooden dormitory (long gone) where the students slept. The park was named for James Henry Roper, who built Gainesville Academy in 1858 and served as its first principal. That school, located on the west corner of West University Avenue and Southwest 2nd Street, was the city's first. In 1866, after the Civil War, the state took over the Academy and made it the East Florida Seminary.

Alachua County officials were so concerned over the education of its citizens that they ordered that the tuition of poor students be paid out of public funds. In those early days the county had only private schools, and only white children could attend. By 1866, the Gainesville Academy had 65 boys and girls attending and a faculty of three. After the Civil War, other schools opened up in the county, including a school for blacks.

Roper was also commemorated in the former name of East 7th Street, but that street, like others in the city, had a number substituted for the name. The park itself was known in the early part of this century as City Park. Another previous name was Barracks Park in honor of the nearby barracks of Gainesville Academy and the fact that the students of the Academy used the park to do their marching.

Northeast 4th Avenue

10. **Gracy House**
314 Northeast 4th Avenue

This beautiful, spacious house in the Colonial Revival style takes its name from its builder, Luther Gracy, a wealthy turpentine dealer, lumberman, and civil leader who handpicked the house's lumber from his own mills around 1906. The 6,000-square-foot house has eight fireplaces and ceilings that stretch sixteen feet from the floor downstairs and eighteen feet in the attic. Porches on the first and second floors extend almost halfway around the outside of the house. A swimming pool in the back adds a modern touch.

The wood used in the building of the interior of the house includes curly pine, heart pine, magnolia, oak, pecan, and rosemary pine. The paneling in the west parlor and in the halls upstairs and downstairs is said to have come from one native cherry tree.

Temperance leader Carry Nation visited the Gracy family here, probably because Mr. Gracy was a well-known prohibitionist. During her visit, she gave the children small wooden axes as a symbol of her determination to destroy alcohol stills around the country. Another visitor was three-time presidential candidate William Jennings Bryan.

The house still retains much of the original design, especially the colonnaded, balustraded verandas and its imposing portico. In 1983, the house was named a Designers' Showcase House to raise funds for the Thomas Center Gardens. Various interior designers decorated the rooms of the old house with the latest in design and fashions. The public was charged a small fee to tour the premises and see the latest in art and interior decorating.

11. McArthur-Graham House
417 Northeast 4th Avenue

The iron fencing and castellated roof with parapets make this Romanesque house especially beautiful. The gothic-looking house has seven fireplaces. The builder of the house, A.J. McArthur, was the city's fire chief at a time when Gainesville had horse-drawn water wagons. A subsequent owner of the house was Klein Graham, the first business manager/auditor for the University of Florida, who began working for UF in 1906, soon after the school moved here from Lake City, and finally retired in 1948. He received much praise for handling the entire budget for the university for many years. Graham added the castlelike parapets and stone porch in 1913, perhaps because he admired similar features on UF buildings.

In 1972, the Jester family bought it and restored it to its original elegance, opening up the formerly enclosed front porch and rewiring the old structure to make it conform to modern codes.

Northeast 5th Avenue

12. Murphree House
306 Northeast 5th Avenue

Albert Alexander Murphree, Sr., who served as president of the university from 1909 to his death in 1927, lived at 306, a large Greek Revival/Southern Colonial–style house built between 1911 and 1913. A.A. Murphree was born in Alabama (1870), studied at Walnut Grove College in Alabama, became a teacher and then superintendent of city schools in Cullum, Alabama (1888). In 1894, he completed his bachelor's degree at the University of Nashville, which later became Peabody College. After two years of teaching mathematics, he became in 1897 president of Tallahassee's West Florida Seminary, which later became Florida State University. In 1909, he became the second president of the University of Florida, which had been moved to Gainesville from Lake City.

The Murphrees entertained many notables in this house. For example, there was William Jennings Bryan, who wanted to nominate Murphree as the Democratic Party's candidate for president of the United States in 1924. However, Murphree refused the honor. The second-floor balcony, which is characteristic of its architectural style, was used by William Jennings Bryan for giving speeches to students and townspeople gathered below. The balcony extends over the veranda and is supported by four paired two-story Corinthian columns.

The next owners were Major and Mrs. Arthur Carlos Tipton, who occupied the house from 1936 until 1942. Tipton, an All-American football player at West Point, became in 1924 Commandant of the University of Florida R.O.T.C., a post he held until he retired in 1936. Subsequent owners divided the three-story house into seven apartments, razed the garage, and built a three-car garage with apartments above. In 1975, designer Bill Warriner bought it and began restoring it to its former elegance.

North Main Street and Northeast District

Murphree House

Duck Pond Area

This area is one of the most sought-after neighborhoods for those who want to live in elegant older homes. The Boulevard area, unlike most of the city's streets, which are laid out in symmetrical patterns, winds around Sweetwater Branch. When the subdivision was built there in the mid–1920s, engineers created a water-retention pond between Northeast 5th and 6th Avenues. That pond, called Vidal's Lake after city commissioner James Vidal, who was in charge of streets when it was dug, soon became the Duck Pond, when ducks were added.

The Duck Pond is the centerpiece of the Northeast Historic District, which was placed on the National Register of Historic Places in 1980. Each spring for the past two decades a group of residents have opened their older homes to the public as part of the city's annual Spring Pilgrimage. As more and more families have chosen to live in this neighborhood and have painstakingly restored the houses to their former splendor, the value of those houses has risen dramatically.

Duck Pond

13. **Farr-Adkins House**
708 Northeast Boulevard

This impressive Colonial Revival house with its three attic dormers and columned portico was built from half of the Thomas dairy barn, which used to supply milk for the White House Hotel on Main Street. The Thomas family's cows used to graze along the Sweetwater Branch in front of today's house.

The Farr-Adkins House was the home (1925–35) of English professor James Farr, one of the early administrators of the University of Florida. He had been head of the Department of English of Florida Agricultural College at Lake City from 1901 until it moved to Gainesville in 1906 and became the University of Florida. At that time, he continued as head of the English Department, but also became Vice President of UF and first coach of the university's football team. When Dr. A.A. Murphree, then-president of the university, died in 1927, Farr was named acting president and held that post until Dr. John Tigert became president in 1928. Farr retired in 1934 and moved to Jacksonville Beach, where he wrote his memoirs.

Farr-Adkins House

In 1936, Farr sold his Gainesville house to James Adkins, owner of a box-manufacturing company. His son, Shelton "Red" Adkins, later became mayor of Gainesville in 1959. The Adkins family lived in the house until 1971, when they sold it to absentee owners, who rented it out to students. It also served as the Loblolly School for local children. In 1980, the Boyd family bought the house and restored it.

Across the Duck Pond at 531 Northeast Boulevard is the **Gehan House**, the home of another English Department professor, Freddie Gehan, and his wife, Clara Gehan, who was the first woman graduate of UF's Law School and one of the city's most distinguished lawyers. The molding at the front of the Cape Cod–style house features country maids and children with musical instruments, a fitting symbol for a professor who taught Children's Literature at UF for many years.

Northeast 6th Avenue

14. Yon-Murphree House
403 Northeast 6th Avenue

Built around 1900, this house was occupied by Everett Yon, who served as athletic director for the university. In 1917, Dr. Albert Murphree, president of the university (1913–27), bought the house to be used as student apartments until the mid-1930s. At that time, it became the residence of his son, "Waddie" Murphree, one of the university's Rhodes Scholars and a long-time member of UF's English Department. In 1986, the McGill family bought it and repaired and restored it. As with many older homes in the Duck Pond area, this house had to be rewired to meet modern codes. Its broad veranda, which extends around much of the house, is particularly noteworthy.

15. Thomas Center
306 Northeast 6th Avenue

From a private residence to a hotel to a community college to a cultural center/city office building, the Thomas Center has had many roles. Restored today to some of its former elegance, the complex of buildings is a popular place for small concerts, conferences, and weddings. The building was begun in 1906 by Charles Chase, president of one of the successful phosphate companies in the area, and then finished in 1910 by William Reuben Thomas for his home. He and his wife and five children lived there for fifteen years. As mayor (1901–07) and an important businessman in Gainesville, Thomas helped convince the Florida legislature to move the University of Florida from Lake City to Gainesville. (The oldest building on the UF campus, Thomas Hall, honors him.) In the late 1920s, architect William Edwards, who also designed several University of Florida buildings, added a three-story wing and transformed the building into the Hotel Thomas (1928–68). The hotel, which had ninety-four guest rooms, three dining rooms, and four lounges, became an important center for cultural and social events of the city.

North Main Street and Northeast District

Thomas Center

Poet Robert Frost (1874–1963) lived at the Brown Cottage behind the hotel when he was in Gainesville. After the hotel closed in 1968, the building was used as the campus of Santa Fe Community College (1968–75) while its campus was being built in the northwest part of the community. Historic Gainesville, Inc., a concerned group of community residents, succeeded in having the Thomas Center listed on the National Register of Historic Places in 1973.

The city of Gainesville bought the property the following year, restored it, and transformed it into a cultural center and city office building. The two handsome buildings that make up the Thomas Center cover 58,000 square feet in the middle of six acres of landscaped gardens. Phone: (352) 334-2197.

Northeast 8th Avenue

16. Citizens Field
Northeast 8th Avenue and Waldo Road

From the 1930s to the 1950s, Citizens Field was the site of baseball games played by the minor-league team called the "G-Men." However, the stadium in those days, called Harris Field after local baseball manager Charlie Harris [(1877–1963), third baseman for the Baltimore Orioles (1899) and manager of the local amateur teams Badgers and the G-Men] was located where the fire station is today.

The G-Men won the Florida State League, Class D minor league pennant in 1949. The pennant race inspired the documentary produced by the local WUFT-TV, "Gainesville Wins the Pennant." Baseball, one of the most popular sports in Gainesville over the years, attracted World Series fans to the area in front of the offices of *The Gainesville Sun* near the old Post Office downtown to listen to radio broadcasts of the inning-by-inning play. Even before then, in the spring of 1919, the New York Giants played the Boston Red Sox (with Babe Ruth) in a pre-season game at Citizens Field. Among the early baseball teams that played in Gainesville were the Oak Halls, the all-black Central City Nine, and the semipro Hav-a-Tampas.

In 1997, at 1028 Northeast 14th Street behind Citizens Field, officials dedicated the **Martin Luther King Jr. Multipurpose Center**, the first city-built recreation center since Westside Park in 1968. Inside is a portrait of Dr. King with excerpts from his most famous speeches.

Northeast 10th Avenue

17. Tigert House
214 Northeast 10th Avenue

This Colonial Revival mansion at the north entrance to the Boulevard area was built in 1929 as part of the Highlands subdivision. The house is noteworthy on the outside for the four white columns at the front and, on the inside, for the main staircase that resembles President George Washington's staircase in his Mount Vernon home. Local builder M.M. Parrish built the seventeen-room house, but lost it in the real-estate bust of the early Depression years. An important road contractor, L.M. Gray, owned it until 1960. The house was rented for many years by the University of Florida, which used it as the official residence of the third and fourth UF Florida presidents, John J. Tigert (1931–47) and J. Hillis Miller (1947–55). (In 1955, UF presidents began living in the newly built presidential home on the campus.)

The 5,500-square-foot house is now the residence of Mark and Mary Barrow, two of the city's most important preservationists. They converted the garage into a guest house and enclosed the side porch with glass to add even more room to the spacious house. Some local children think that the creaks and groans one can sometimes hear in the old house are the sounds that the ghost of Dr. Tigert is making as it wanders through the hallways.

18. Gainesville Regional Airport
East of Waldo Road

Airplanes began servicing the Gainesville area in the early 1920s. Expansion of the university soon necessitated an airport, so in 1930, local officials purchased 150 acres northeast of the city and began building an airport. Today that site is east of Waldo Road (State Road 24) and north of Northeast 39th Avenue (State Road 222).

In the early 1940s, the Army and Navy Air Forces used the Gainesville airport for pilot training and spent a good deal of money to upgrade the facilities. We can still see, to the east of the present airstrip, grass-covered roads and the concrete slabs that marked the foundations of barracks and office buildings of the former Alachua Army Air Base built there in World War II.

In 1948, the military field ceased operations, and the field was returned to the city. Later, the city added more buildings and improved facilities. Eastern Airlines brought the first jet service to town in 1971. By the 1990s other airlines, for example, US Air and Delta, had begun using the airport.

At one point, the airport was heated and cooled by one of the largest solar facilities in the country for a commercial building.

V.
NORTHWEST DISTRICT

Northwest 1st Street

THE FIRST AFRICAN AMERICANS PROBABLY CAME TO ALACHUA County as slaves in the 1800s, although such records are scarce today. By 1860, according to census figures, forty-six blacks (17% of the total population of 269) lived in Gainesville, many of them probably slaves. Ten years later, the blacks outnumbered the whites, 765 to 679, partly because many black soldiers were stationed there in the Civil War. Men of the Third Regiment, one of the Union's all-black regiments, remained in the area after the war and were joined by recently freed slaves.

This part of Gainesville, bounded today by Northwest 1st Street, Northwest 8th Avenue, Northwest 6th Street, and Northwest 2nd Avenue, is known as The Pleasant Street Historic District. After the Civil War, it became the primary area in the city where blacks settled, many of them bakers, carpenters, realtors, and tradesmen from Camden, South Carolina. Some of them, especially farmers and ranchers, settled in the towns of Freedom and Monteocha north of Gainesville, but the artisans and other skilled workers moved into Gainesville. There, African Americans built more than two hundred houses, stores, schools, and at least three churches. Skilled workers found jobs in town and moved their families to what they hoped would be a thriving commercial town. As in many towns and cities in the South, including Florida, African Americans tended to congregate together for protection and mutual support and were, in fact, limited as to where they could settle.

Because education was such an important goal in the lives of African Americans in Gainesville, the Freedman's Bureau built the Union Academy in 1866 on what is now the southwest corner of Northwest 1st Street and

V. NORTHWEST GAINESVILLE

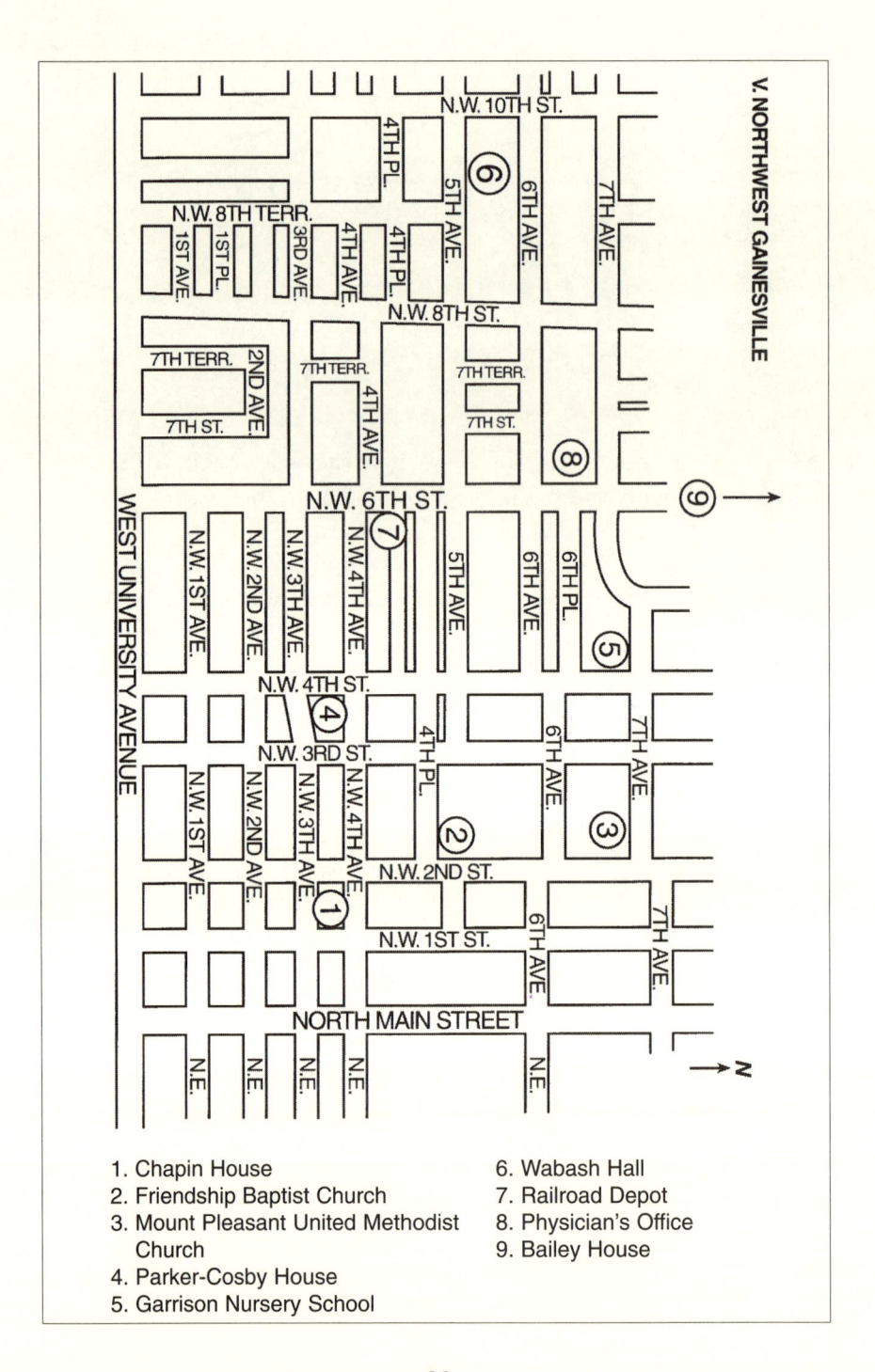

1. Chapin House
2. Friendship Baptist Church
3. Mount Pleasant United Methodist Church
4. Parker-Cosby House
5. Garrison Nursery School
6. Wabash Hall
7. Railroad Depot
8. Physician's Office
9. Bailey House

6th Avenue. The land for the school was purchased by black citizens of Gainesville, who helped build the wood-frame school and made up the Academy's Board of Trustees. At first, white teachers from northern states, much resented by the white population of the town, taught the hundred or more students. But, in time, black teachers, some trained at the Union Academy, were teaching classes so large the school had to be enlarged in 1899 to contain them.

By that time, the Union Academy had 500 pupils, many from rural areas who boarded in town while they went to school. A. Quinn Jones was the last principal of the Union Academy and, when a new two-story red brick school for the black students was built in 1923 in the 1000 block of Northwest 7th Avenue, Professor Jones, as he was known, headed that school until his retirement in the 1950s. This handsome building with Italian Renaissance features is now known as the A. Quinn Jones Center.

Gainesville integrated its public schools in 1970 with relatively few instances of violence. One year before that, Neil Butler was elected to the City Commission and thus became the first African American to be a city official since the 1800s. Butler became mayor in 1974, the first time an African American had reached that post since Josiah Walls in 1876.

Butler and other city commissioners passed an ordinance that prohibited discriminatory practices on the basis of race, religion, sex, marital status, or physical handicap. Since that time, other African Americans like Charles Chestnut III, Cynthia Chestnut, Ed Jennings, and Rodney Long have been elected to political office, a fact that has encouraged more and more African Americans to become involved in the running of the city and county.

In the 1990s, Gainesville's black community represented about twenty percent of the city's population. By contrast, blacks make up about twelve percent of the total U.S. population and fourteen percent of Florida's population. And while blacks were formerly concentrated in the Northwest 5th Avenue and Southeast section past Waldo Road, today they are spread throughout the city. Many, but not all neighborhoods, have been integrated with very few incidents of racial harassment. Still, almost seventy percent of the city's black population is concentrated in three districts: the historically black Northwest 5th Avenue and two others east of Waldo Road, north and south of East University Avenue. Each of these districts is more than eighty percent African-American.

GAINESVILLE

1. **Chapin House**
   320 Northwest 1st Street

Built in 1886 by J.C. Chapin, the house was later converted into apartments, but eventually deteriorated to the point where officials condemned it and prepared to raze it. Local preservationists Sande and Keifer Calkins bought it in 1984 and restored it, adding a beautiful two-story front porch and winning a 1988 Florida Trust award for the restoration. The house is called "Rosewood" because much of the interior wood was burled heart pine or "rosewood." The building today houses Warrington's Fine Interiors, a decorating service for residential and commercial customers. The Italianate architectural style stresses balance and symmetry of floor plan and window arrangement, as well as ornate eave brackets.

Northwest 2nd Street

Formerly called Pleasant Street, this thoroughfare had just north of this church **Cato's Drug Store**, **Dr. P.M. Stafford's Office**, **Johnson Hall** (where plays for Union Academy took place), and businesses that allowed the African Americans to stay in the area and not have to venture outside, where they might not be welcome. Even when the white-owned stores downtown would sell food and soft drinks to African Americans, those customers had to buy them at the back door or the far end of the lunch counter and remain outside to eat or drink.

North of **Dorsey's Funeral Home**, which used to be **White-Jones Funeral Home**, at 727 Northwest 2nd Street is the site of the former **Metz Theatre** that African Americans attended.

Another church in the area was **Old Mount Carmel Baptist Church** at 429 Northwest 2nd Street. The building itself was constructed in the late 1940s. The churches in the black community became an important focal point during the civil rights movement of the 1960s. Secret societies like the Ku Klux Klan and the Young Men's Democratic Club tried to harass African Americans in the 1950s and 1960s and, in many instances, committed acts of violence against African Americans, including the burning of churches.

Listed on the National Register of Historic Places in 1989, the Pleasant Street Historic District is undergoing restoration and revitalization.

2. Friendship Baptist Church
426 Northwest 2nd Street

This is one of the important churches in the black community. Originally built in 1888, the building was destroyed by fire in 1911. The congregation then built the present structure, a Romanesque Gothic Revival church with rusticated concrete block. Of particular significance are the many stained-glass windows that ring the outside of the building. Today, the Pleasant Street Historical Society meets in the church building as it plans to restore old structures and bring back a sense of pride to the community.

This church and Mount Pleasant United Methodist Church each received the 1997 Matheson Award from the Matheson Historical Center

Friendship Baptist Church

as having contributed significantly to the preservation of the history and heritage of Alachua County.

3. Mount Pleasant United Methodist Church
620 Northwest 2nd Street

This church serves the oldest black congregation in Gainesville, dating back to 1867, just after the end of the Civil War and the same year that the Freedman's Bureau established Union Academy in the area. In 1883, Reverend Isaac Davis and nine trustees paid $160 to Charles Brush for the lot that the church sits on. They then built a wooden church which soon became a religious center for the black community for decades. Mount Pleasant was a member of the South Carolina Annual Conference until the organization of the Florida Annual Conference took place in 1873.

In 1887, the parishioners laid the cornerstone for a new brick structure. That building and a nearby parsonage were destroyed by fire in 1903. A year later, the congregation laid the cornerstone for the present red brick Romanesque-Revival–style building, the oldest intact church building in Gainesville, having been completed in 1906. Particularly noteworthy are the church's turn-of-the-century stained-glass windows, its two-and-a-half-story tower with stained-glass fanlight, and architectural detailing found in Victorian buildings.

Northwest District

Mount Pleasant United Methodist Church

Northwest 4th Street

Northwest 4th Street, originally called Grove Street, still has descendants of some of the original settlers in the area.

4. Parker-Cosby House
303 Northwest 4th Street

Built around 1877, this two-story frame house was the birthplace and office of Julius Parker, one of the city's first black doctors and owner of the Parker Drug Company. Dr. Parker was born in Gainesville in 1877, attended Meharry Medical College in Nashville, started a medical practice in Oklahoma in 1902, and later moved back to Gainesville to minister to the needs of the sick.

He became president of the Citizens Alliance, a group of people dedicated to establishing a recreational center at the site of old Union Academy. Dr. Parker's house later became the residence of his daughter, Julia, and her husband, Dr. Edgar Cosby, a dentist.

Another doctor in the area was Dr. A.B. Ayer, who built a house at 511 Northwest 2nd Street and practiced medicine north of Mount Pleasant Church, as well as having an office downtown.

Houses in this neighborhood were also used to house black chauffeurs who drove wealthy white visitors to town in the early decades of this century. The black drivers were not allowed to stay in the whites-only hotels, but had to stay in the black neighborhoods.

5. Garrison Nursery School
626–628 Northwest 4th Street

This nursery school was built in the mid-1930s during the Depression, with Works Progress Administration (WPA) funds. The school was operated by Bessie Marie Garrison, an enterprising lady who also ran a boarding school for young women, including those students from outlying areas who wanted to attend school in this area.

Garrison Nursery School

Northwest 5th Avenue

This avenue, which used to be known as Seminary Street, was the center of African American life in the 1940s. Among the popular stores were **Cato's Sundry Store** for snacks, at 737 Northwest 5th Avenue; **Walter's Blue Room** for dancing, at 912 Northwest 5th Avenue; **Plummer's Barber Shop** at 743 Northwest 5th Avenue; and the **Lincoln Theater** for movies, in the 400-block of Seminary Street. Today, a barbershop/cab shop is where the theater used to be. Since 1980, residents have hosted the Fifth Avenue Arts Festival, an annual weekend celebration that features artists and performers. The festival attracts over twenty thousand visitors.

Although many African Americans continued working on local farms during Reconstruction and into the twentieth century, others chose to have their own businesses, many of them on Pleasant Street. Some worked as cooks, waiters, porters, and drivers, and a few became doctors, teachers, and lawyers.

World War I had relatively little effect on most African Americans in Gainesville, although the economy of the city did improve and many young men were drafted into the Army. A bigger change occurred with the outbreak of World War II. Once again, many African Americans were drafted into the Army, and many young soldiers, black and white, were stationed at Camp Blanding, about twenty-five miles north of Gainesville.

That base housed 25,000 soldiers. On weekends, many of the African American soldiers stationed there came to Gainesville to unwind and find some relaxation from the rigors of military training. Local businesses that catered to the African American soldiers prospered. After the war, many of those African American soldiers, especially those who had fallen in love with local women, returned to Gainesville to settle down and raise their families.

6. **Wabash Hall**
Just east of the corner of 10th Street

Typical of the buildings that have graced Northwest 5th Avenue is Wabash Hall, an old, red brick structure that dates back to around 1932 and used to be the scene of music groups like the "Sweethearts of Rhythm," an all-female black band that played from the 1930s to the 1950s. In the days of segregation, Wabash Hall, which has been compared to New York City's Apollo Theater in terms of its local influence, was one of the few local places available for blacks to have dances and proms. Lincoln High School and other clubs would rent out the hall and invite big-name black bands from around the state and South. Performers like Ella Fitzgerald and Cab Calloway used to perform in Wabash Hall. After the Hall closed in 1950, the upstairs was converted into apartments.

Wabash Hall was in the center of several businesses on Seminary Street. To the east of Wabash Hall were Lincoln Theater, Lincoln Grill, and Glover and Gill Grocery, all of which have long since gone.

Northwest 6th Street

7. Railroad Depot
410 Northwest 6th Street

Railroads have had a major impact on the history of Gainesville. The importance of the railroad to Gainesville can be seen in the official city seal, which has a locomotive over the date "1869" (the date of the town's incorporation) surrounded by the corporate name: "City of Gainesville" and "State of Florida." When the first railroad came through in 1859, Gainesville was well on its way to becoming a major town of north central Florida.

The railroad became somewhat of a liability in February 1864, when Union troops marched down the tracks to raid Gainesville. Confederate troops turned them back, but more Union troops came in August of that year for another attack. In that foray, the Union had fifty-two soldiers killed and three hundred wounded, while the Confederates had only eight men killed or wounded.

After the Civil War, the railroad continued serving Gainesville for passenger traffic and for transporting crops to northern markets. Carl Weber's book, *The Eden of the South*, predicted in 1883 that Gainesville would eventually become the railroad center of the state. Although that did not happen, Gainesville did become the place where tracks of different gauges met.

Before the railroad companies established a standard gauge for their tracks, three different-size tracks met at Gainesville: the three-foot gauge of the Florida Southern; the four-foot gauge of Henry Plant's Savannah, Florida and Western line; and the five-foot gauge of the Transit line. Gainesville became the place where cargo was switched from one line to another.

The railroads also played a part in the 1888 yellow fever epidemic that ravaged Florida. Local officials placed "shotgun quarantine" guards at the town's railroad depots to check the health certificates of arriving passengers. Later, around 1900, the railroads offered half-price fares to anyone who would settle in Florida.

The Seaboard Coast Line built the depot on Northwest 6th Street in 1948, when the railroad tracks on Main Street were torn up. For many years

Railroad Depot

the depot served the one northbound and the one southbound freight train that came through each day. As people relied more and more on the automobile, train traffic decreased in Gainesville just as in other cities around the United States. When the railroad stopped using the tracks that parallel Northwest 6th Street, Santa Fe Community College took over the depot, converted it into a downtown campus in 1988, and expanded in 1993 by adding the nearby Gainesville Gas building for classroom use.

8. Physician's Office
635 Northwest 6th Street

The physician's office at this site on 6th Street (formerly called Alabama Street) was where Dr. Cullen W. Banks practiced medicine for almost five decades. A year after Dr. Banks received his medical degree from Howard University in 1948, he assumed the practice of Dr. Orien Ayers. Dr. Ayers, like the two other black general practitioners at that time in Gainesville, Drs. H. Floyd and J.A. Parker, had not been given privileges at Alachua General Hospital (AGH). Dr. Banks later became the first black physician to have full privileges at AGH and was the only black family physician in private practice in town until about 1980. When he retired in 1995, Dr. Donna Hunt of Baltimore took over his practice.

The city has come a long way from as recently as forty years ago when

Alachua General Hospital would allow African American patients to be treated only on the fourth floor of the hospital. When the beds were filled on that floor, the patients were put in the hall, not in a room on another floor. And they would still be charged for a room.

9. Bailey House
1121 Northwest 6th Street

The oldest house still standing in Gainesville today was built in 1854 by Major James Bailey. Major Bailey owned a cotton plantation, sixty acres of which he sold for the new town of Gainesville soon after its establishment in 1853. Preservationists restored the frame vernacular residence in the 1980s and made it into an attractive retirement home with four acres of shaded yard and garden.

VI.
WEST UNIVERSITY AVENUE AND NORTHWEST 13TH STREET

West University Avenue

1. Gainesville National Bank Building
2 West University Avenue

The wooden structures built here in the 1880s included the Arlington Hotel, a three-story building that could accommodate 200 guests in the fashionable winter season. Such notables as Teddy Roosevelt and General Ulysses S. Grant stayed here at a time when Gainesville was the fourth largest city in Florida. However, after an 1884 fire burned down both this block and the block just to its south, builders began using masonry for new buildings. The new brick building was originally a dry goods and clothing store; in 1907, it became the Gainesville National Bank; from 1924 to 1982, a Woolworth's department store; and finally a furniture store and restaurant (1990s). The second floor housed the Gainesville Guards Armory during the late nineteenth and early twentieth centuries. For many years in the early part of this century, this block was the most valuable business site in the city.

2. Dutton Bank Building
20–22 West University Avenue

This large brick building, built in 1885 as the Dutton Bank, housed one of the earliest private banks in Florida. It also served as the head office of the H.F. Dutton Company, which was Gainesville's chief mercantile company in the late nineteenth and early twentieth centuries. From the 1870s until 1910, Dutton, which manufactured the Doig Cotton Gin, was the major ginner of Sea Island cotton, which was produced in the county.

VI. WEST UNIVERSITY AVENUE and NORTHWEST 13TH STREET

WEST UNIVERSITY AVENUE:

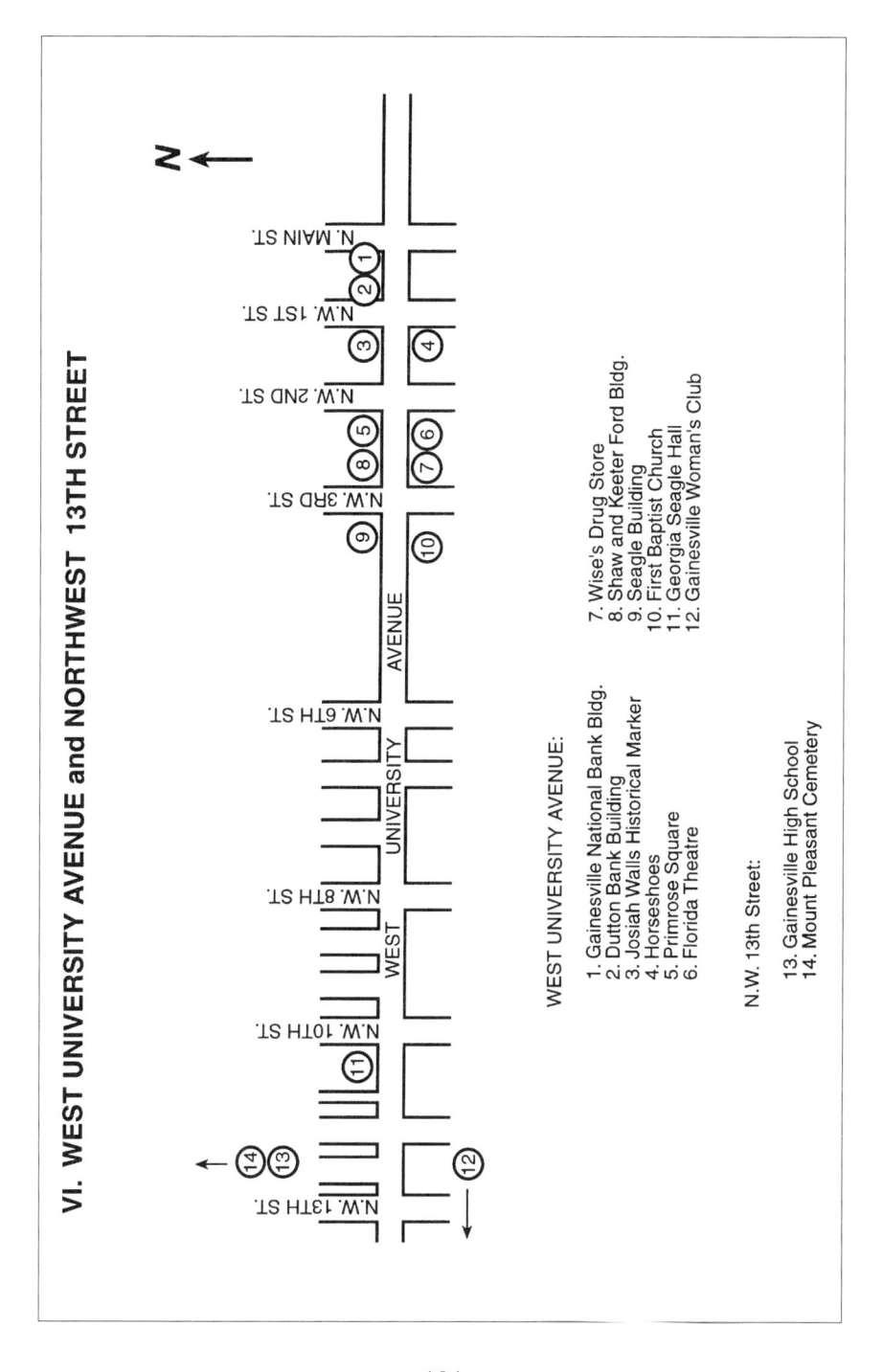

1. Gainesville National Bank Bldg.
2. Dutton Bank Building
3. Josiah Walls Historical Marker
4. Horseshoes
5. Primrose Square
6. Florida Theatre
7. Wise's Drug Store
8. Shaw and Keeter Ford Bldg.
9. Seagle Building
10. First Baptist Church
11. Georgia Seagle Hall
12. Gainesville Woman's Club

N.W. 13th Street:

13. Gainesville High School
14. Mount Pleasant Cemetery

GAINESVILLE

Gainesville National Bank Building

Dutton Bank Building

W. University Avenue and N.W. 13th Street

Beginning in 1891, the H.F. Dutton Phosphate Company consolidated the phosphate-mining operations in the county. The phosphate shipped to Europe from Alachua County from 1895 to 1898 made up approximately half of the entire U.S. phosphate production. In 1914, the Gainesville National Bank absorbed the Dutton Bank, which had been established in 1873 by Col. H.F. Dutton, long considered the town's greatest businessman. In 1888, builders increased the height of the building from two to three stories. The Masonic Lodge used the third floor for meetings until they built their own lodge in 1908. Secret societies used that meeting space until 1922, after which it was left vacant. The second floor was used as professional office space.

3. Josiah Walls Historical Marker
On the corner of West University Avenue and Northwest 1st Street

This marker honors Josiah Walls (1842–1905), the first black congressman from Florida. Although Walls was born in Virginia, he fought in the Civil War in Florida on the Union side. After the war, he moved to Jacksonville, then to Archer, Florida, where he worked as a lumberman and teacher before being elected to Florida's House of Representatives (1868) and the state Senate. He was then elected to the U.S. Congress and served three terms (1870–76). For two years (1873–74) he operated a Gainesville newspaper, the *New Era*, the first Florida newspaper owned by a black. He later joined Matthew Lewey in publishing the *Farmer's Journal*. Walls served as mayor of Gainesville in 1873, then went to Tallahassee to work as the director of the farm at Florida Normal College, which later became Florida A&M University. This great man, who is buried in the Negro Cemetery in Tallahassee, was the last black to represent Florida in the U.S. House of Representatives until the 1992 election.

4. **Horseshoes**
Just off West University Avenue on Southwest 1st Street

The horseshoes in the sidewalk on the west side of Southwest 1st Street (formerly South Garden Street) between West University Avenue and Southwest 1st Avenue recall a time when a wagon-and-buggy shop stood at 20 Southwest 1st Street. The horseshoes headed toward that shop as an advertisement for it and for a blacksmith shop that operated at 103 Southwest 2nd Place.

Primrose Square

5. **Primrose Square**
214 West University Avenue

Having served originally as a private home for a university professor (1910), this building was renovated and opened as The Primrose Inn and Grill (1924). It closed its lodging facilities in the early 1960s, but remained a popular eatery and meeting place. After it closed in 1988, it became an office complex known as Primrose Square.

6. **Florida Theatre**
233 West University Avenue

This two-story brick building, which was Gainesville's main movie theater for about forty years (1920s–60s), has been restored and is used today for musical shows and bands. Formerly known as the Great Southern Music Hall, the eight-hundred-seat building was built in 1928 and had as its first show the movie *The Four Walls*, one of the first "talkies" and starring John Gilbert and Joan Crawford. In the days of the silent films, theater employees would perform live sound effects like the revving of a car engine. The

Florida Theatre

live trees that were planted in the organ lofts at the front of the auditorium made the thirty-foot screen over the stage look like a moon rising over a jungle.

Vaudeville troupes performed there, as well as performers like Dave Brubeck, Jose Feliciano, Waylon Jennings, and Melissa Manchester. The rise of television and the poor quality of movies hurt the popularity of the theater, although some young moviegoers seemed to revel in the poor movies. To make their point about how bad a movie was, the rowdy youngsters would tear off the arms of the seats and throw them at the screen. Until desegregation finally tore down the barriers of racism, African Americans were not allowed to go to the Florida Theatre, but could only attend the Lincoln Theater on Northwest 5th Avenue.

The theater closed in 1974 and opened in the same year as the Great Southern Music Hall. Popular singers like Tom Petty and Willie Nelson performed there. In 1990, the upholstered seats were removed to make room for a dance floor as the theater adjusted to the changing interests of its clientele, many of whom were college students.

GAINESVILLE

7. Wise's Drug Store
239 West University Avenue

This popular downtown site, which was founded in 1938 by Joe Wise, Sr., has been on the Southwest 200 block since the 1930s and at this location next to the Florida Theatre since 1958. It has been a popular place for lunch for many years, especially as other eateries downtown have closed. It is the only soda fountain left in Gainesville.

8. Shaw and Keeter Ford Building
238 West University Avenue

The large building across the street from Wise's Drug Store has seen several major businesses: Shaw and Keeter Ford Company (1930s); Nichol's Alley, a large disco with a tunnel of flashing lights for an entrance (1970s); the Lone Star, a country-music dance hall; the Islands, a Caribbean club (1980s); Skeeter's, a country-type restaurant famous for its "Big Biscuit" (1990s); Gator Bumpers, a recreation hall for bumper cars (1990s); and most recently, a gathering place for eating and dancing.

W. University Avenue and N.W. 13th Street

9. Seagle Building
408 West University Avenue

Planned as a luxury hotel, the Dixie (or Kelley) Hotel, begun in 1927 during the state's land boom, became the victim of the 1920s real estate bust and remained unfinished. Georgia Seagle finally had the eleven-story building, the city's second tallest building (after UF's Beaty Towers), finished in 1936, renamed it in honor of her brother, and gave it to the University of Florida to house the Florida State Museum.

The UF Department of Engineering used the top floors for classified research funded by the Department of Defense after World War II, and the Division of General Extension used the seventh, eighth, and ninth floors for their work.

After the museum was moved to the university campus, real estate developers spent four million dollars in 1983 renovating the Seagle Building. The top floors became luxury condominiums, with offices on the middle floors and the Heritage Club restaurant on the bottom two floors. Above the sixteen condominium apartments on the sixth through tenth floors is the eleventh-floor penthouse, a luxurious suite with three bedrooms, two bathrooms, living room, fireplace, dining room, and two thousand square feet of living space.

The Seagle Building was placed on the National Register in 1982.

Early days of the Seagle Building

Florida State Archives

10. First Baptist Church
425 West University Avenue

The Baptists of Gainesville have a long history, going back to 1870, when Rev. J.H. Tomkies organized a twenty-one-member congregation. Five years later, they built a church at the corner where South Main Street and Southeast 2nd Avenue are today. In 1897, the congregation needed a larger building and thus built a brick church on the corner of East University Avenue and Northeast 2nd Street, a site later used by the First Christian Church and now by the City Hall.

In 1921, the congregation bought the land where the present church stands on West University Avenue, and in 1924 held the first services in the new building. Beginning in 1948, a growing membership necessitated establishing a number of missions around town. Those missions have since become self-sufficient Baptist churches.

The West University building, which represents the Classic Revival Architecture style, has six tall pillars at the front and beautiful woodwork inside for a congregation of more than a thousand worshipers.

W. University Avenue and N.W. 13th Street

11. **Georgia Seagle Hall**
1002 West University Avenue

The three-story colonial home several blocks east of the University of Florida campus is a cooperative living center. Male college students, in exchange for working on various house maintenance jobs there, can live much less expensively at Seagle Hall than if they had to pay a typical apartment rent. The students live in their own rooms, but share the bathroom, recreation, living, and dining areas.

The building was built in the mid-1930s. In 1938, its owner, Georgia Seagle Holland, used the building to house the UF football team. When the players returned to living on campus the following year, she operated the building as a boarding house. When Ms. Holland died in 1943, her trust named the Florida Conference of the United Methodist Church as trustee. Ms. Holland's will stipulated that the building be a nonsectarian Christian facility that provided financial assistance to UF students in need. The Methodist Church operated the building through the 1970s, after which it was administered by a local bank. When the bank later tried to sell the property, many of the 1,000 men who had lived there over the years formed an alumni association that preserved the facility.

12. **Gainesville Woman's Club**
2809 West University Avenue

In 1895, members of several community women's clubs met in Green Cove Springs, Florida, and organized themselves into the Florida Federation of Women's Clubs (FFWC). This organization was founded for the betterment of communities, and has established libraries, hospitals, and other community facilities.

In 1903, the Gainesville Woman's Club (GWC), originally named The Twentieth Century Club, was established. The first initiation fee was twenty-five cents and its dues were fifty cents. In 1904, the club joined the FFWC. In 1960, it changed its name to the Gainesville Woman's Club.

The GWC's first fund-raiser was for the purpose of buying books for what would become the city's first public library. In 1915, the club won a Carnegie grant to build the city's first library building. The club later established the Friends of the Library group, which holds two book sales each year to raise money for library book purchases. The GWC's first clubhouse was opened in 1921 at 700 West University Avenue, but later moved to Northwest 16th Boulevard, where the Gainesville Community Playhouse is now located. In 1958, the club bought five acres on West University Avenue and moved into its present building in 1961.

Over the years, besides helping establish and support libraries, the club has been involved in various community projects, such as the city's first hospital (Alachua General), Ronald McDonald House, Hope Lodge, the Matheson Historical Center, and Altrusa House.

Gainesville Woman's Club

Northwest 13th Street

13. **Gainesville High School**
1900 Northwest 13th Street

The first Gainesville High School (GHS) building was a twelve-room structure on University Avenue built in 1905. Seven years later, officials added an auditorium and twelve classrooms. In 1919, GHS had its first student government; a year later, it had its first student newspaper. Two years later, the school was moved further west to 723 West University Avenue. In 1920, voters passed a bond issue to build two new public high schools in Gainesville, Lincoln High School for black students (the present A. Quinn Jones Center) and Gainesville High School for white students. Its principal in the 1930s was Prof. F.W. Buchholz, a former Rhodes Scholar and football coach who set high standards for his students. GHS moved into its present location in 1957.

The school was integrated in January 1970, when a federal judge desegregated schools and Lincoln High School was closed. That integration had begun slowly in 1965, when one black student from each of Lincoln High School's three grades was admitted to GHS.

14. **Mount Pleasant Cemetery**
Between Northwest 29th Road and Northwest 30th Avenue

The small cemetery (established in 1886) on the east side of Northwest 13th Street is a five-and-a-half-acre plot that holds much history for Gainesville's black community. Among the important African Americans buried there are the town's first two black doctors (Dr. R.V. Ayers and Dr. Julius A. Parker), the first black dentist (Dr. E.H. DeBose), the first soldier from Gainesville to die in the Vietnam War (Lance Corporal Vernon T. Carter, Jr.), even the great-grandparents of singer Leslie Uggams. Mount Pleasant United Methodist Church (630 Northwest 2nd Street), one of the town's oldest black churches, owns the cemetery.

VII.
OUTLYING AREAS

Northwest 16th Boulevard

1. Gainesville Community Playhouse
4039 Northwest 16th Boulevard

This regional theater was established as the Gainesville Little Theater in 1927 by Mrs. F.W. Buchholz (the wife of a prominent Gainesville educator) and has been in its present location since 1961. It is the longest continuously running theater in Florida. In its early years, the theater put on four plays each season in places like the auditoriums of the P.K. Yonge Laboratory School and Gainesville High School. In 1961, S.T. Dell Jr. and his sister, Mrs. Hal Mordock of Miami, donated the building, which had been the home of the Gainesville Woman's Club, to the theater in memory of Eloise Zellar, an active participant in the theater. Phone: (352) 376-4949

Other cultural groups in Gainesville include Dance Alive!, a professional-level dance company; Dans-company; Gainesville Ballet Theatre; Gainesville Civic Chorus; Gainesville Chamber Orchestra; and Gainesville Symphony Orchestra.

VII. OUTLYING AREAS

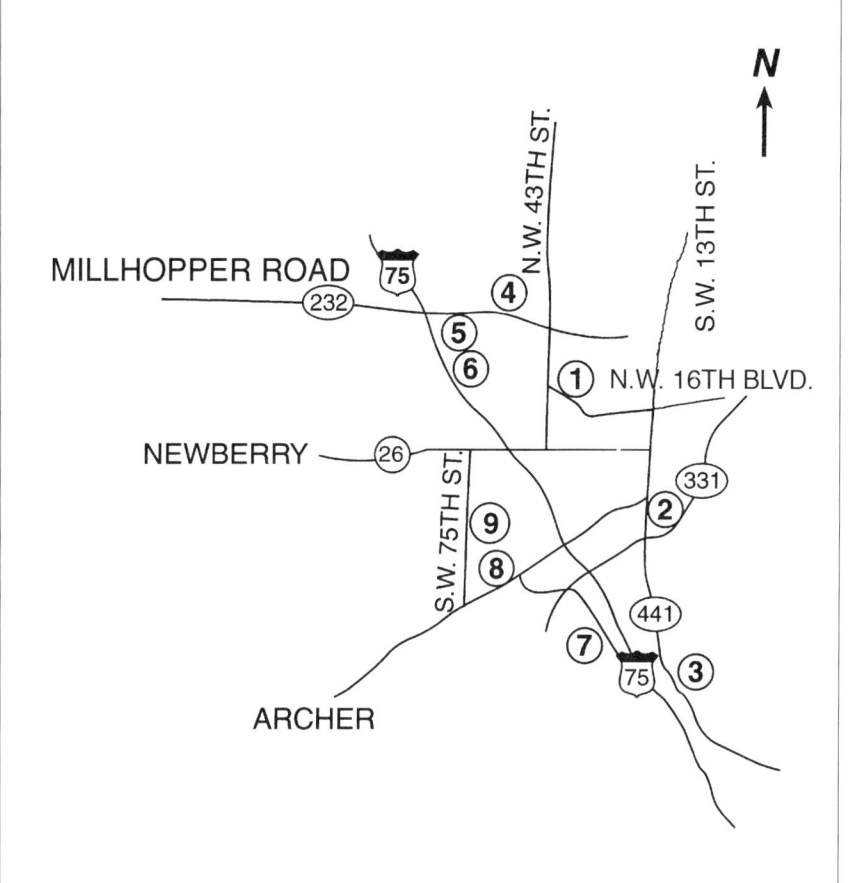

1. Gainesville Community Playhouse
2. Bivens Arm Nature Park
3. Paynes Prairie
4. Devil's Millhopper
5. San Felasco Hammock State Preserve
6. Santa Fe Community College
7. Fred Bear Museum
8. Kanapaha Botanical Gardens
9. A Walk Through Time

Southwest 13th Street

Southwest 13th Street has student apartments, many restaurants and motels, and the Bivens Arm Nature Park. As you drive under the old railroad bridge just below the turn-off to Archer Road, notice the wall on the left, which has a mural on it to replace the unsightly graffiti that used to mar the wall. The old railroad bridge has been caged for the safety of bicyclists using it. Gainesville has many such bikeways and bike lanes on most of the major roads, all of which has made the city a safer place to bicycle. The city also has a rails-to-trails bikeway that goes along Paynes Prairie from Boulware Springs to the nearby town of Hawthorne.

2. Bivens Arm Nature Park
South Main Street

Near the intersection of Waldo Road and Southwest 13th Street, with its main entrance on South Main Street, is a nature park opened by the city in 1984. The park's lake was once part of Alachua Lake in Paynes Prairie, which formed when Alachua Sink was plugged with debris and the prairie filled with water. When the sink was unplugged and the Alachua Lake drained, the lake in this nature park remained full of water. Today the park has a long boardwalk and trails through the natural terrain.

Outlying Areas

3. Paynes Prairie

Just south of the city lies Paynes Prairie State Preserve, twenty thousand acres of marsh and pasture where alligators, bald eagles, deer, turkeys, and sandhill cranes, and countless species of wildlife live. There are even buffalo, brought in from Oklahoma. About ninety thousand visitors a year visit the prairie to camp, swim, go on ranger-led walks, see the many displays at the Visitor Center, and take advantage of several tall observation decks.

Named for Seminole Indian Chief, King Payne, the prairie has had as some of its main residents many Florida scrub cattle. those animals were the direct descendants of the cattle that the Spanish brought to this land in the 1500s. Visitors to the wooden boardwalk off Highway 41 may see some of the wildlife that roam over the prairie.

Environmentalists have restored much of the park to the condition in which famed explorer William Bartram saw it in 1774. The basin of Paynes Prairie, about eight miles long and four miles wide, used to be full of water to a depth of several feet. From 1871 to 1891, the basin had so much water from a plugged-up sinkhole that "Alachua Lake" had small steamboats operating on it. Phone: (352) 466-3397.

Paynes Prairie State Preserve

4. Devil's Millhopper
4732 Northwest 53rd Avenue, formerly called Millhopper Road

This enormous sinkhole, one of the county's most famous landmarks, attracts about fifty thousand visitors a year. When the state's Park Service acquired the site in the mid-1970s from the University of Florida, it was designated a "State Geological Site," the only one in Florida at the time.

The sides of the sinkhole, which is 120 feet deep and 500 feet across, are covered with thick vegetation. The sinkhole, which formed between fourteen thousand and twenty thousand years ago, resulted from the collapse of a roof of a cavern, which formed from the erosion of underground limestone deposits.

In 1976, workers built a 221-step wooden stairway so visitors could reach the bottom without having to climb down the slippery slopes and cause damage to the fragile environment.

The sinkhole takes its name from its shape, which resembled the funnel-shaped hopper used in old mills to feed grain into grinders to make meal. The "Devil" part of the name may come from an old belief that sinkholes were caused by the Devil trying to escape from the earth, or to get more people into his domain.

The sixty-three-acre park has oak hammocks and upland pines, and has a walkway through the trees. A visitors' center at the park entrance has exhibits of fossil shark teeth and marine shells from a time when the ocean covered Florida. Hours: 9 A.M.– sunset. Admission charge.

Outlying Areas

5. San Felasco Hammock State Preserve
Millhopper Road

Further out on Millhopper Road, three and a half miles west of the Devil's Millhopper on State Road 232, lies San Felasco Hammock. The name goes back to the mispronunciation of the name "San Francisco" by Indians and other early settlers. This was the site of the Spanish mission called San Francisco de Potano. The Florida militia had a brief skirmish there with the Seminole Indians during the Second Seminole War.

This 6,500-acre preserve has an abundance of natural flora and a sample of most major forest types in north Florida, as well as numerous ponds, streams, and marshes. Evidence from artifacts indicates that Indians inhabited the area from at least 8000 B.C. In 1974, the state purchased the area under Florida's Environmentally Endangered Lands Program, primarily because of the rich diversity of geological features and plant communities.

Among the wild animals one can see are bobcat, gray fox, white-tailed deer, and turkey. Environmental scientists train here in ecology and wildlife.

The Preserve attracts about twelve thousand visitors a year. There are self-guided walks or ranger-led hikes and horseback rides, including guided overnight hikes and overnight horseback rides into the preserve. Phone: (352) 336-2008. Millhopper Road.

Bike Paths

There are many bike paths in and around Gainesville, and Millhopper Road has one of the best in the area.

6. Santa Fe Community College
3000 Northwest 83rd Street

The Florida legislature established Santa Fe Community College (then called Santa Fe Junior College) in 1965. Its first president was Joseph Fordyce.

The college has had several homes over the years. Its first location was at the former Buchholz Junior-Senior High School (since torn down) on West University Avenue. In the 1970s, it relocated to the former Hotel Thomas in northeast Gainesville.

In 1972, under its second president, Alan Robertson, the northwest campus opened on 175 acres next to Interstate 75. Since then the college has established branch campuses at the old Bradford County Courthouse in Starke (1986) and the old train depot on Northwest 6th Street in Gainesville (1990). The depot has been renamed the Charles L. Blount Downtown Center, after the owner of several automobile dealerships and one of the developers of Haile Plantation.

Larry Tyree became SFCC's third president in 1990.

When classes were first offered in September 1966, fewer than one thousand students enrolled. Today more than twelve thousand students take credit classes, and another twenty thousand take non-credit classes.

Outlying Areas

The Teaching Zoo on the campus is the only community college teaching zoo in the United States. It houses many kinds of animals, birds, and endangered species from around the world. Phone: (352) 395-5604.

The college has hosted an annual Spring Arts Festival in downtown Gainesville since 1970.

7. **Fred Bear Museum**
Archer Road (Exit 75) at I-75

Here one can see mounted brown bear, cape buffaloes, elephants, lions, and wolves, as well as authentic spears, shields, artwork, and Indian artworks, many of them collected by Fred Bear, expert bow-hunter. Open Wednesday–Sunday, 10 A.M.–6 P.M. Closed Christmas Day. Admission. Phone: (352) 376-2411, ext. 5.

GAINESVILLE

8. **Kanapaha Botanical Gardens**
4625 Southwest 63rd Boulevard

This beautiful sixty-two-acre garden off Archer Road can be reached via I-75, exit 75. The garden has meadows, woodlands, and specialized gardens full of butterflies, hummingbirds, and wildflowers. There are many kinds of flowers, Florida's largest bamboo collection, a water-lily pond, fern grotto, and sunken garden. Admission fee. Phone: (352) 372-4981.

9. **A Walk Through Time: Kanapaha Park**
Tower Road and Southwest 41st Place

This monument was raised to commemorate the men and women from Alachua County and the University of Florida who died in wars defending freedom around the world. The granite, brick, and tile berm walk, where one linear foot equals one year in time and each brick represents one thousand total casualties suffered during military action, spans 219 feet and covers ten wars, from the Revolutionary War through Desert Storm. Inscribed on a plaque at the base are the names of known Alachua County soldiers killed in each war. Handicapped accessible. Open twenty-four hours a day, seven days a week. Free.

Outlying Areas

Kevin McCarthy and his son, Matthew, stand before the Civil War plaque.

FURTHER READING

"Alachua County's courthouse." *The Gainesville Sun*, August 18, 1985, p. 8G.

"Alachua memorial asked as role for old courthouse tower clock." *The Florida Times-Union* [Jacksonville], June 21, 1961, p. 29.

Lars Andersen. *Paynes Prairie: A History of the Great Savanna*. Sarasota: Pineapple Press, 1998.

Bob Arndorfer. "Hangin' at Lynch Park." *The Gainesville Sun*, February 18, 1996, p. 1Dff.

Bob Arndorfer. "New use for old space" [about the Cox Warehouse]. *The Gainesville Sun*, June 19, 1994, p. 1Fff.

Bob Arndorfer. "Turning a new page" [about the new library]. *The Gainesville Sun*, February 3, 1991, p. 1Dff.

Bob Arndorfer and Doris Chandler. "Crossing the divide" [about racial incidents in Gainesville]. *The Gainesville Sun*, October 8, 1989, p. 1Dff.

"Bailey houses [sic] shares history." *The Gainesville Sun*, May 22, 1983, p. 14E.

Mark V. Barrow, Sr. "Early history of medicine in Alachua County." *Journal of the Florida Medical Association*, vol. 69, no. 8 (August 1982), pp. 670–80.

George Bayliss. "The old clock, 99 years old, is ticking again." *The Gainesville Sun*, March 31, 1984, p. 1ff.

Mike Bianchi. "The G-Men." *Sports 2* [Gainesville], February 24, 1994, p. 4ff., esp. p. 18 [about the Central City baseball team].

Mark Bondurant. "Elegance restored" [about the Baird House]. *The Gainesville Sun*, June 16, 1991, p. 1Fff.

Fritz W. Buchholz. *History of Alachua County, Florida, Narrative and Biographical*. St. Augustine: The Record Company, 1929.

Mike Carter. "Cotton and the Dutton Bank." *The Numismatist*, July 1979, pp. 1438–1443.

Daniel G. Cassidy. *The Illustrated History of Florida Paper Money*. Jacksonville: Daniel G. Cassidy, 1980, pp. 74–78 [about Gainesville banks].

Doris Chandler. "A medical trailblazer." *The Gainesville Sun*, July 23, 1995, p. 1Aff.

GAINESVILLE

Doris Chandler. "Porter's residents focus on future." *The Gainesville Sun*, July 23, 1989, p. 1Fff.

"The changes in city hall since 1927." *The Gainesville Sun*, April 7, 1985, p. 10G.

Maurine Christopher. *Black Americans in Congress*. New York: Thomas Y. Crowell Company, 1976, pp. 78–86: "Josiah T. Walls/Florida."

Church of the Holy Trinity: A Panorama of Our Parish. Compiled by the St. Elizabeth and St. Margaret Circles, Holy Trinity Church. Gainesville: Holy Trinity Episcopal Church, 1991.

Barney Colson. "Street where the boys were" [about East University Avenue]. *North Florida Living*, May 1985, pp. 42–43.

Betty Cortina. "Saving Seagle Hall." *Today* [UF magazine], February 1993, pp. 14–17.

Jess G. Davis. *History of Alachua County*. Gainesville: 1960.

Jess G. Davis. *History of Gainesville, Florida, with Biographical Sketches of Families*. Gainesville: no publisher, 1966.

Bill DeYoung. "The Devil's Millhopper." *The Gainesville Sun*, October 16, 1990, p. 1Dff.

Sam Dolson. "When The Babe came to Gainesville." *Sports 2* [Gainesville], February 24, 1994, p. 3ff.

"5th Avenue: It's where the action is." *The Gainesville Sun*, February 27, 1972, p. 6Eff.

"First Baptist fetes 91st anniversary." *The Gainesville Sun*, October 15, 1961, p. 29.

"First of the fire trucks" (with a photo). *The Gainesville Sun*, May 4, 1969, p. 5A.

"Florida's lifestyle homes." *Florida Living*, vol. 9, no. 9 (September 1989), pp. 4–5, also the cover.

Michael Flynn. "It wasn't easy being a fireman in the early days." *The Gainesville Sun*, December 1, 1974, p. 2C.

Barbara Foster. "Family's loving restoration returned home's past beauty." *The Gainesville Sun*, March 9, 1986, p. 1Dff.

Barbara Foster. "Gainesville finds a water source." *The Gainesville Sun*, March 2, 1980, p. 11E; continued on March 9, 1980.

Barbara Foster, "Progress severs Alachua County's link to the past." *The Gainesville Sun*, Sept. 13, 1981, p. 7E.

Al Hall. "This old house" [about the McArthur-Graham House]. *The Gainesville Sun*, February 24, 1974, p. 1F.

Further Reading

Nancy Dohn Gholz. "Couple's teamwork restores home of first UF president" [about the Murphree House]. *The Gainesville Sun*, November 16, 1986, p. 1Cff.

Michael Gowan. "First Baptist to celebrate 125 years." *The Gainesville Sun*, August 12, 1995, p. 6Dff.

Polly J. Haines. "Alachua Army Air Field." *The Gainesville Sun*, October 1, 1995, p. 1Dff.

"Hallowed history" [about Mount Pleasant Cemetery]. *The Gainesville Sun*, July 26, 1986, p. 1Bff.

Thornton Hartley. "Gainesville's seedy old Fire Station No. 1 getting last call." *The Florida Times-Union*, April 9, 1962, p. 20.

Merrily Helgeson. "Rebirth of the old depot." *The Gainesville Sun*, January 14, 1989, p. 1Aff.

James Hellegaard. "Selling alternatives to college proves to be a formidable task." *The Gainesville Sun*, "Business Monday" section, September 2, 1991, p. 6ff.

James Hellegaard. "SFCC center brings hope to downtown." *The Gainesville Sun*, January 24, 1993, p. 1Bff.

Charles H. Hildreth and Merlin G. Cox. *History of Gainesville, Florida, 1854–1979*. Gainesville: Alachua County Historical Society, 1981.

"Historic Gainesville" [about Kirby Smith School]. *The Gainesville Sun*, January 29, 1984. P. 11E.

Carol Hole. "This new chapter inspires look back on library's history." *The Gainesville Sun*, February 3, 1991, p. 2D.

Aaron Hoover. "It's the tops" [about the penthouse apartments in the Seagle Building]. *The Gainesville Sun*, November 12, 1995, p. 1Fff.

Wilhelmina W. Johnson. *The History of Mount Pleasant United Methodist Church through the Years: 1867–1985*. Gainesville: no publisher, 1985.

John Paul Jones. "Downtown renaissance." *Guide to North Florida Living*, vol. 3, no. 6 (November–December 1983), pp. 29–41.

John Paul Jones. "Sweetwater Branch." *Guide to North Florida Living*, vol. 1, no. 1 (May–June, 1981), p. 28ff.

John Paul Jones. "Upside down mountain." *North Florida Living*, January 1984, pp. 40–42.

Gary Kirkland. "Homes are part of city's history" [about the Southeast Historic District]. *The Gainesville Sun*, February 15, 1988, p. 1Bff.

Mindy Klein. "Harris Field making way for future." *The Gainesville Sun*, February 6, 1987, p. 6D.

Peter D. Klingman. *Josiah Walls*. Gainesville: University Presses of Florida, 1976.

Charlie Kroll. "Chief Bear" [about Bear Archery]. *Guide to North Florida Living*, vol. 1, no. 2 (July–August 1981), pp. 24–25.

Murray D. Laurie. "Evergreen Cemetery." *The Album* [a publication of the Matheson Historical Center, Inc.], vol. 1, no. 1 (January 1995), pp. 1–4.

Murray D. Laurie. "The Union Academy: A Freedmen's Bureau school in Gainesville, Florida." *Florida Historical Quarterly*, vol. 65, no. 2 (October 1986), pp. 163–74.

"Matheson Historical Center." *Florida Living*, vol. 10, no. 1 (January 1990), pp. 48–50.

"Matheson House is city's 2nd oldest." *The Gainesville Sun*, June 12, 1983, p. 14E.

Kevin M. McCarthy. *Baseball in Florida*. Sarasota: Pineapple Press, 1996.

Judy McKnight. "A fire station was born in 1869." *The Gainesville Sun*, October 14, 1966, p. 6.

Linda Miklowitz. "Seagle Building: White elephant gets reprieve." *The Gainesville Sun*, Oct. 22, 1973, p. 8B.

Derrick Morgan. "African-Americans have rich past in Gainesville." *The Gainesville Sun*, February 27, 1994, p. 1Aff.

Derrick Morgan. "G-Men bring their baseball memories." *The Gainesville Sun*, July 24, 1994, p. 1Bff.

Mary Newell. "Along the Avenue" [about East University Avenue]. *The Gainesville Sun*, March 26, 1989, p. 1Fff.

Peggy O'Neal. "Gainesville Plaza home for old buildings." *The Florida Times-Union* (Jacksonville), July 1, 1976, p. 1B.

Joe Padilla. "'A bicycling mecca.'" *Adventures Quarterly*, summer edition, May 20, 1995, p. 22.

Ben Pickard. "The Baird House & family," *Matheson Historical Center, Inc., Newsletter*, vol. 3, no. 2 (February 1993), pp. 1–3.

Ben Pickard, editor. *Historic Gainesville: A Tour Guide to the Past*. Gainesville, Fl.: Historic Gainesville, Inc., 1990.

Ben Pickard. "The Kirby Smith struggle." *Preservation in Progress*, vol. 17, no. 4 (June 1988), pp. 1–3.

Ben Pickard. "The Lambreth-McKenzie house," *Matheson Historical Center, Inc., Newsletter*, vol. 3, no. 1 (October 1992), p. 1ff.

Ben Pickard. "Salvation: The Hodges house." *Gainesville Today*, December 1994, pp. 12–14.

Further Reading

Ben Pickard. "The Swearingen-Austin house," *Matheson Historical Center, Inc., Newsletter*, vol. 4, no. 2 (January 1994), pp. 1–3.

John B. Pickard. *Florida's Eden: An Illustrated History of Alachua County*. Gainesville: Maupin House, 1994.

Ann C. Pierce and Germaine Warmke. "Hiking a San Felasco Hammock Trail." *Guide to North Florida Living*, vol. 1, no. 3 (September–October 1981), pp. 13–14.

"Pony-riding Irishman led Presbyterians here." *The Gainesville Sun*, April 19, 1969, p. 8.

Bob Pulley. "The 'forgotten neighborhood' fights back." *The Gainesville Sun*, August 19, 1990, p. 1Dff.

Frank Rathbun. "A Clock for the times," *North Florida Living*. vol. 4, no. 2 (February 1984), pp. 14–15.

Frank Rathbun. "Gainesville—The Bicycle City." *Today In Gainesville*, November 1982, p. 6ff.

Frank Rathbun. "New look for Paynes Prairie." *Guide to North Florida Living*, vol. 2, no. 2 (March–April 1982), pp. 18–21.

Frank Rathbun. "Sanctuary" [about Morningside]. *Guide to North Florida Living*, vol. 1, no. 1 (May–June, 1981), pp. 36–39.

Frank Rathbun. "Santa Fe Teaching Zoo." *Today in Gainesville*, January 1984, p. 8ff.

Mary Richardson. "Family's love saves craftsman's bungalow from time's decay" [about the restoration of the Fagan House]. *The Gainesville Sun*, November 28, 1982, p. 1G.

Mary Richardson. "Final duck pond 'disaster' restored to former beauty" [about the Jordan House]. *The Gainesville Sun*, December 11, 1983, p. 1Gff.

Mary Richardson. "Florida Theatre." *The Gainesville Sun*, December 29, 1985, p. 1Bff.

Mary Richardson. "'Imaginative rehabilitation' brightens two downtown buildings." *The Gainesville Sun*, May 29, 1983, p. 1G.

Mary Richardson. "Pleasant Street." *The Gainesville Sun*, February 16, 1986, p. 2Eff.

Jeanne Rochford. "Woman's club marks milestone." *The Gainesville Sun*, February 15, 1995, p. 1Dff.

Terry Lee Rogers. "Gainesville's progress seen in city hall history." *The Gainesville Sun*, April 13, 1969, p. 7A.

GAINESVILLE

Cissy Steinfort Ross. "Rails once ran down Main into the city's heart and history." *The Gainesville Sun*, July 7, 1974, p. 4E

Marlyn Rubin. "Baptists have deep roots in city's history." *The Gainesville Sun*, April 12, 1969, p. 8.

Marlyn Rubin. "Same synagogue scene of worship 45 years ago." *The Gainesville Sun*, April 19, 1969, p. 8.

"Santa Fe Community College." *The Gainesville Sun*, April 20, 1986, p. 11Gff.

Mitch Stacy. "Bivens Arm litter patrol." *The Gainesville Sun*, June 14, 1993, p. 1Dff.

Mary Shedden. "Local historians chronicle black cultural experience." *The Gainesville Sun*, February 26, 1995, p. 1Aff.

David Sowell. "Racial patterns of labor in postbellum Florida: Gainesville, 1870–1900," *The Florida Historical Quarterly*, vol. 63, no. 4 (April 1985), pp. 434–44.

Colee Splichal. "A dream realized" [about the building of the library]. *The Gainesville Sun*, March 11, 1990, p. 1Fff.

Julie Stricker. "Step into the past" [about the Southeast Historic District]. *The Gainesville Sun*, April 9, 1988, p. 1Dff.

"Tabernacle housed chautauqua events." *The Gainesville Sun*, December 15, 1985, p. 16G.

Cheryl W. Thompson. "Pleasant Street's star rising." *The Gainesville Sun*, May 17, 1989, p. 1B.

Cheryl W. Thompson. "Recalling the days of Union Academy." *The Gainesville Sun*, February 18, 1989, p. 1Aff.

Nat Tillman. "Trip to 5th Avenue rolls back years to the '40s on Seminary." *The Gainesville Sun*, Sept. 24, 1980, p. 1B.

"Wabash Hall is quiet now." *The Gainesville Sun*, February 27, 1972, p. 3E.

Margaret Warrington. "Prejudice, envy stalk shopping center for blacks." *The Gainesville Sun*, February 27, 1972, p. O12.

"The Waterworks at Boulware Springs served Gainesville." *The Gainesville Sun*, April 29, 1984, p. 10E.

"When John, the fire horse, retired." *The Gainesville Sun*, June 1, 1969, p. 9A.

"Yesterday and tomorrow." *The Gainesville Sun*, Sept. 29, 1990, p. 8A.

Ross A. Zito. "How we built a nature park" (about Bivens Arms Nature Park). *The Longleaf Pine* [publication of the Morningside Nature Center], November 1984, p. 6ff.

PART TWO

University of Florida

Murray D. Laurie

A BRIEF HISTORY OF THE UNIVERSITY OF FLORIDA

In September 1906, when the first students arrived at the newly established University of Florida in Gainesville, the 102 young men encountered conditions that students of today would find amazing. There were just two unfinished, all-purpose red brick buildings, Buckman and Thomas Halls, rising in Gothic splendor from a landscape of dusty paths, isolated sinkholes, tall pines, and newly planted oak trees. The University had a faculty of sixteen professors, the students wore uniforms, and tuition was free for Florida residents. (Out-of-staters paid $20.) Far in the future were air conditioning, a football stadium, computer terminals, and parking garages.

The town of Gainesville and the campus were decked out in orange and blue when the University was formally dedicated on September 27. One speaker at the ceremony predicted that future UF graduates would include governors, senators, judges, and many others who would make important contributions to the state of Florida, and in time this prophesy did come true.

Campus traditions evolved along with the University's curriculum. For example, the alligator became the logo of the football team and *The Alligator* was chosen as the title of the campus newspaper; freshmen wore orange and blue beanies, or "rat caps," as they were called; a small museum showed off fossils and Indian relics in Science Hall (now Flint Hall), where classes in physical and life sciences probed new research horizons; and the first Homecoming, in 1924, was kicked off with a parade down University Avenue.

In imitation of older universities, a variety of types of ivy was introduced to cover the walls of the new buildings. In 1927 a campus landscape plan was drawn by the well-known firm of Frederick Law Olmsted Jr., designer of New York's Central Park. In 1931, UF President John J. Tigert dedicated the central quadrangle as the Plaza of the Americas and had representatives from the nations of the Americas plant trees as a gesture of hemispheric good will.

In addition to keeping up their grades and cramming for exams, students managed to relax and have fun. Fraternities hosted parties and dances (strictly chaperoned), the Glee Club and Gator Band performed at concerts and football games, the Dramatic Club recruited faculty wives and young ladies from the Gainesville community as honorary members, and everyone looked forward hopefully each fall to a successful football season.

During World War I, a battalion of some four hundred men moved on campus for Army training. In October of 1918, a Spanish influenza epidemic struck the campus, overwhelming the capacity of the small wooden infirmary. The Depression of the 1930s that followed Florida's 1920s real estate boom slowed the construction of new buildings, and meant that the splendid University Auditorium, begun in 1924, would remain unfinished for another fifty years.

After World War II, the population of the campus exploded. Hastily erected temporary classrooms and living quarters popped up like mushrooms after an autumn rain. Campus demographics also altered. Married students, some with children in tow, took advantage of the GI Bill and enrolled by the thousands.

Although women had been admitted to the all-male University of Florida under special circumstances since 1925, in 1947 the Florida legislature ended the official segregation of the sexes. By 1949 more than two thousand women students had enrolled. Women living on campus observed a strict curfew and a dress code that prohibited shorts and jeans, but they had a definite advantage in the dating game with the overwhelmingly male student body.

In 1949 the University of Florida was designated as the site of the state-funded medical school and teaching hospital. The large complex of buildings devoted to the healing arts was established in the southeast corner of the campus, named as a memorial to UF President J. Hillis Miller.

"Bricks-and-mortar" could have been the theme of the 1950s on the UF campus as the various colleges expanded programs. With generous federal grants the University put up more and more classrooms, laboratories, and offices. The visual symbol of the UF campus, the Century Tower, was built in the 1950s. Funding was also secured for dormitories, with those for men built on the west side of the campus and those for women on the east.

The more permissive 1960s ended this segregation when residence halls became coed, and many students adopted the hippie lifestyle, taking part in antiwar rallies, demonstrations, and sit-ins.

The trend toward an ever-larger student body was moderated somewhat during the 1980s. However, it picked up momentum in the 1990s, with a current enrollment of approximately forty thousand. Trying to find a parking place on campus has become one of campus life's greatest challenges.

Despite the burgeoning student body and a parallel increase in building that goes along with it, the campus has retained its pleasant ambiance. Plantings of azaleas blaze forth in the spring; there are quiet courtyards, grassy plazas, and patches of woodland; and the many giant oak trees, some planted in 1906 on the raw ground of the new campus, provide welcome shade under their canopy. The collection of nineteen Collegiate Gothic buildings built between 1906 and 1939 was listed as a historic district on the National Register of Historic Places in 1989, and this part of the UF campus has also been designated a Florida Heritage Landmark.

In ninety years, the University of Florida has become an outstanding research institution, ranked among the top public and private universities in North America as a member of the prestigious Association of American Universities.

But, of course, many students and alums probably consider the ranking of the Florida Gators in 1996 as the nation's number one football team a more dazzling symbol of the University of Florida's place in the sun.

AREA 1

1. Century Tower
Stadium Road and Newell Drive

Ground was broken for the Century Tower in 1953. The Tower commemorated the centennial of the University of Florida, based on the founding dates of the earlier colleges that had been combined to form UF in 1905 and honors those students who gave their lives in World War II. It also pays homage to the original design of architect William A. Edwards in the early 1920s, which called for a Gothic tower with chimes as the focal point for the university campus.

The carillon atop the Century Tower is more than a set of bells. It is a magnificent musical instrument and a symbol of cultural unity on the cam-

The center of campus in 1947, before the Century Tower was built
Florida State Archives

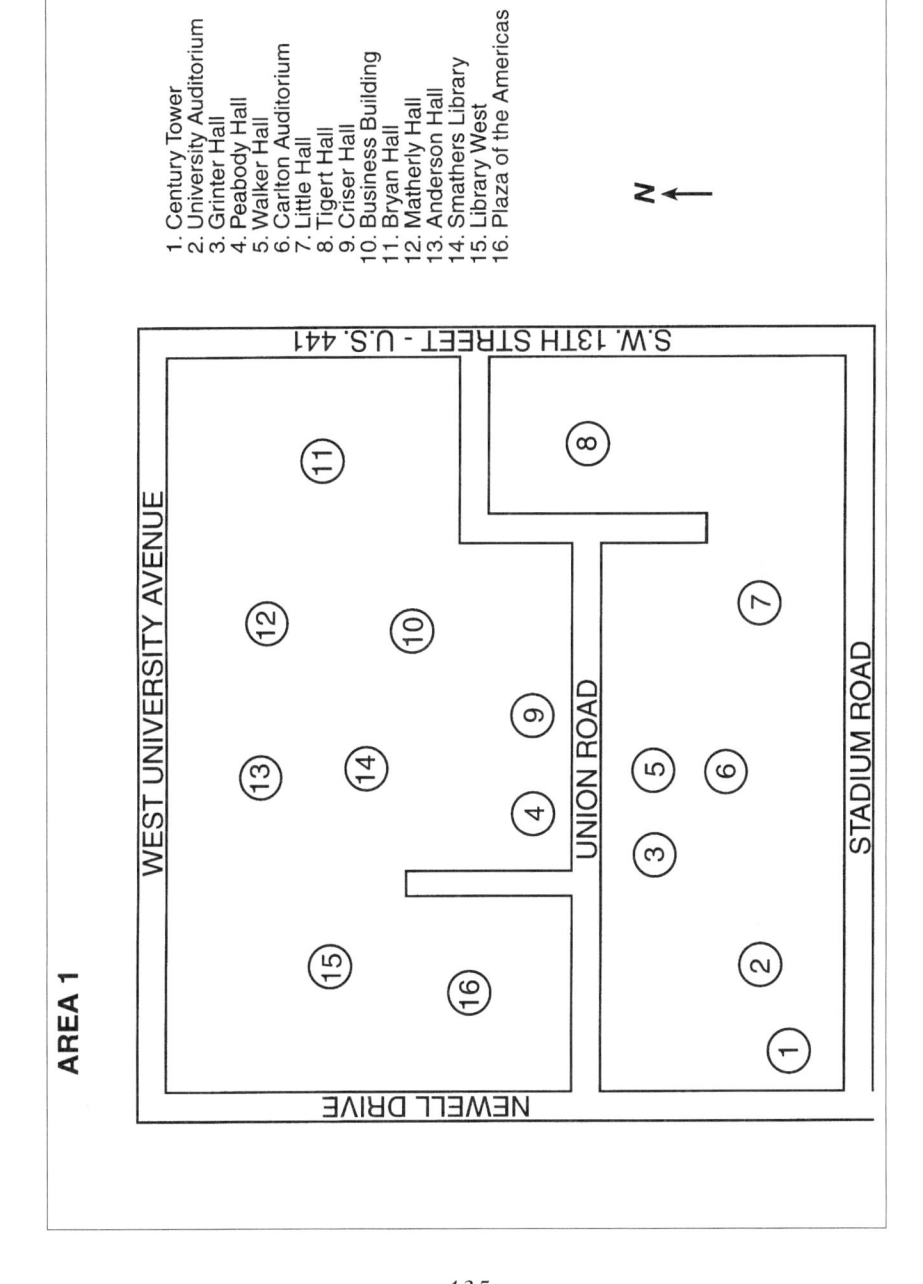

AREA 1

1. Century Tower
2. University Auditorium
3. Grinter Hall
4. Peabody Hall
5. Walker Hall
6. Carlton Auditorium
7. Little Hall
8. Tigert Hall
9. Criser Hall
10. Business Building
11. Bryan Hall
12. Matherly Hall
13. Anderson Hall
14. Smathers Library
15. Library West
16. Plaza of the Americas

pus. Its mission is to "call together those who are studious of all good things both human and divine." Forty-nine bells herald occasions of importance and ring out noontime concerts of seasonal music, original compositions, classical favorites, and pop tunes—for instance, "Raindrops Keep Falling on My Head" chimes out on rainy days.

The carillonneur must climb 194 steps within the 157-foot tower to reach the instrument's keyboard, located in a small room just below the bell chamber, to play the bells, each of which is hung individually. The largest bell, which is five feet tall and weighs seven thousand pounds, is embossed with the seal of the University of Florida. The bells, built and installed by a Dutch firm in 1979, replaced the electronic chimes that had tolled the hours since 1956 when the Tower was completed.

On those rare occasions when the Tower is open to the public, it is worth the climb to enjoy the magnificent bird's-eye view of the campus.

A favorite campus myth is associated with the Tower: A brick is supposed to fall from the Tower if ever a virgin passes by.

2. University Auditorium
Union Road and Newell Drive

This Gothic-style campus landmark was to be the first phase of a grandiose administration building with a soaring 190-foot central tower. The Grand Master of the Masons of Florida laid the cornerstone in 1922, and Governor Cary Hardee addressed the festive crowd, but state allocations could not match the majesty of President Albert A. Murphree's dream and architect William Edwards' original design.

The auditorium wing, in which chapel services were held, stood unfinished for decades, but still functioned as the "heart of the campus." The whimsical gargoyles, representing science, the arts, academics, and athletics, at the ends of the great ceiling beams overlooked performances by guest artists such as John Philip Sousa and Tennessee Williams, lectures by Helen Keller, readings by Robert Frost and Marjorie Kinnan Rawlings, and countless student shows and graduations. The grand organ was installed in 1925, a gift from Dr. James Anderson of St. Augustine.

UF President Stephen O'Connell, who often spent his lunch hour listening to the university choir practice, blocked a move to demolish the venerable building in the 1970s; instead, the towering spire and ornate vaulted ceilings were restored and a new entrance and lobbies added to the

Area 1

north end. This graceful blending of the traditional and contemporary architectural styles was designed by Gainesville architect James McGinley.

The University Auditorium has appeared in major motion pictures (*Parenthood* and *Just Cause*) and is the favorite backdrop for UF students' family-and-friends photographs on graduation day.

University Auditorium

3. Grinter Hall
Union Road

Characterized by abstract classicism and refinement of detail, the stately modern building east of the University Auditorium is named for Linton E. Grinter, Dean of the Graduate School from 1952 until 1969. Dean Grinter secured federal funding for the construction of the new center for the Graduate School and international studies. This building was completed in 1971, on a site formerly occupied by the first home of the College of Engineering, Benton Hall, and dedicated in 1974. The four-story brick building houses the Graduate School and Division of Sponsored Research (now combined as the Office of Research, Technology, and Graduate Education), as well as the Centers for Latin American and African Studies.

A professor of civil engineering, Dean Grinter felt that all students should become involved with the arts and humanities. He insisted that space be set aside in the main lobby for the Grinter Gallery, where changing exhibits of cultural and artistic work could be shown. An abstract stainless steel sculpture by former UF art professor Geoffrey Naylor is positioned over the main entrance, and quotes by Socrates, Tennyson, Bacon, and Wells are inscribed on the walls of the recessed front porch.

Grinter Hall

4. Peabody Hall
Union Road

In 1913, a major gift of $40,000 from the George Peabody Foundation helped complete the forerunner of the UF College of Education. Peabody Hall is one of the four original academic buildings that formed "the quadrangle," an open square with sidewalks connecting Peabody, Floyd, Flint, and Anderson Halls, which was later defined as the Plaza of the Americas.

During the summer months, teachers from all over Florida studied here, earning degrees and certification, and bringing the first coeds to the UF campus. Peabody Hall featured a modern psychology laboratory, and later, when the College of Education moved to the P.K. Yonge Laboratory School (now Norman Hall), other departments held classes in the building. *The Florida Alligator* was printed in the basement, which had also served as the UF library until the first library building was completed in 1925.

Peabody Hall was renovated in 1990 and linked to the new Criser Hall on its east facade. Although the original interior spaces have been altered, the architectural features of the exterior, dignified wall dormers adorned with stone shields, exuberant spires and crockets (those projecting leafy ornaments), and the Gothic lettering over the arched front entry, "George Peabody Hall for the Teachers College," have been preserved. A bronze statue of the University's second president, Albert A. Murphree, is the centerpiece of the landscaped patio north of Peabody Hall.

Statue of President Murphree near Peabody Hall

UNIVERSITY OF FLORIDA

5. Walker Hall
Union Road

Walker Hall was one of the first campus buildings designed by Rudolph Weaver, the successor to William Edwards, the first UF architect. The hall was built in 1927 as the Mechanical Engineering Building, standing to the east of the main College of Engineering building, Benton Hall. (Benton was demolished in the late 1960s. Grinter Hall was built on its site.) The Mechanical Engineering Building was renamed to honor Colonel E. S. Walker, a professor who taught both civil engineering and military science and tactics.

Walker Hall served for many years as an engineering laboratory. It contained boilers, steam and oil engines, refrigeration apparatus, and dynamo equipment on which students could get hands-on training in practical engineering techniques and theory.

The one-story entrance vestibule with arched opening and the parapeted wall dormers distinguish the front facade of the two-and-a-half-story

Walker Hall

red brick building. The elaborated brickwork of the chimney is particularly attractive.

In the 1970s, Walker Hall was renovated and adapted for the use of the Department of Mathematics. Later, a one-story addition was added to the east, enlarging the ground floor space that is devoted to heating and cooling machinery maintained by the UF Physical Plant Division.

Walker Hall now houses the Offices of Academic Support and Institutional Services, Criminology, and Jewish Studies.

6. **Carlton Auditorium**
   Stadium Road

The one-story teaching auditorium, which follows a subtle classical style, was designed by Board of Control architect Guy Fulton. Completed in 1954, it accommodated the steady growth in the student population, particularly those in the University College division, which included all freshmen and sophomore students at that time.

The east portico of the building with its covered porch and stylized pillars and arches faces Little Hall across a paved plaza, a tree-shaded space where students study, chat, and snack between classes. The 680-seat auditorium was named in 1970 for William G. Carlton, a popular and highly respected professor of history and social sciences for over thirty years (1926–62). Known as "Wild Bill" Carlton, his freshman class in "American Institutions" was standing-room-only, the students spellbound by his colorful oratorical style.

Carlton Auditorium

7. Little Hall
Stadium Road

Built in the mid-1960s as the home of University College, Little Hall has a modern design. Its red brick walls are braced by buttresses of concrete aggregate that sweep from the ground level to the flat roofline. University College, or "General College," was initiated in 1935, during John J. Tigert's presidency. It was intended to be a two-year, lower division of the University of Florida, providing general courses in a broad range of subjects, and drawing its faculty from all of the University's colleges and professional schools. It was dissolved in 1977. Winston W. Little, for whom the building was later named, was dean of University College from 1937 until 1964.

Most of the rooms in Little Hall open onto the balconies that wrap around the upper floors and shade the corridors on the ground level. An arched open space reaching to the third floor cuts through the center of the rectangular building.

The Department of Mathematics has recently moved into the third and fourth floors of Little Hall, and a variety of subjects are taught in the classrooms and lecture halls on the first two floors. Some of the larger rooms are equipped to provide computer assisted, multi-media lectures. A popular feature of the tree-shaded plaza west of Little Hall is the "little round house," where drinks and snacks are available during the day.

Little Hall

Area 1

8. Tigert Hall
Southwest 13th Street

Even though it was not built in the heart of the campus facing the Plaza of the Americas as originally planned, the new administration building was described in the *Florida Alligator* as the centerpiece of the campus when it opened in 1950. It was the largest building so far, with 80,000 square feet of space.

Ten years later, the building was named for Dr. John J. Tigert, UF president from 1928 to 1947. Dr. Tigert was a big man with a resounding voice and a rare combination of intellect, athletic prowess, and leadership ability, and during his tenure UF made rapid strides in gaining a position of prominence.

With such progressive features as air conditioning and a computer room (the first on campus) for the registrar, Tigert Hall made a strong transitional architectural statement. While it follows the prevailing Collegiate

Tigert Hall in 1960
Florida State Archives

Gothic style with its red brick walls, stone trim, gabled dormers, bay windows, balustrades, and a red tile roof, the building is contemporary in its expansive glassed entrance pavilion adorned with the UF Seal and in the stylized treatment of the inserts of stone plaques representing the various colleges. The four-story brick building was designed by architect Jefferson Hamilton to be modern and functional, particularly on the interior, yet it contributes to the overall unity of the campus architectural style.

Until Tigert Hall was completed, the offices of the president, vice president, registrar, business manager, and dean of the Graduate School were all located in Anderson Hall.

9. **Criser Hall**
Union Road

The Marshall M. Criser Student Services Center is the realization of a plan to consolidate the Registrar's Office, the Admissions Office, Financial Aid, Student Accounts, Student Counseling Offices, and Student Services, which used to be scattered from one end of the campus to the other.

The four-story contemporary building, which was dedicated in 1991, respects the architectural character of the Collegiate Gothic style, and blends with the historic 1913 Peabody Hall, to which it is linked.

Criser Hall is named for the eighth UF president (1984–89), Marshall M. Criser, who spent six years on campus as a student, working his way through school and earning degrees in business administration and law. Criser later served on the Board of Regents for ten years.

Centered in the symmetrical east facade of Criser Hall is the entrance to the Admissions Office, which is reached through a gabled archway into a spacious lobby. On the lobby's far wall is a shimmering panel of aluminum and glass, "Light Abacus I," by Dale Eldred. Here, new and prospective students come for information and orientation.

On the west side of Criser Hall, which is distinguished by a series of copper canopies placed along the facade and an open plaza, are the UF registration and financial facilities. The recent initiation of the "Telegator" system of phone-in registration has been a great help in this process, and will mean fewer trips to Criser Hall in the future.

Area 1

Criser Hall

10. Business Building

The Business Building, the home of the Fisher School of Accounting (named for benefactors Frederick and Patricia Fisher), forms a hollow triangle. On the exterior facades of the three-story modern classroom and office building, concrete bands separate horizontal dark-glass window walls on two long sides. The shorter west facade is of solid brick with a continuation of concrete bands. Open passageways cut through the building at the ground level, leading to the inner courtyard, where a wide brick stairway rises to the second-floor administrative offices. The building also contains classrooms, research centers, and a computer facility.

Just to the north of the Business Building is the Emerson Courtyard (named for benefactors William and Jane Emerson), built in 1988 as a unifying plaza for the three separate Warrington College of Business Administration buildings that surround it: Bryan Hall, Matherly Hall, and the Business Building. The brick planters with their ivy and azaleas, and the paved walkways, picnic benches, and shade trees make this courtyard an outstanding feature of the main campus.

11. Bryan Hall
Southwest 13th Street

Built in 1914 as the College of Law, a title that is inscribed in Gothic lettering over the west entrance, Bryan Hall is now part of the Warrington College of Business Administration. Named for U.S. Senator Nathan P. Bryan, first chairman of the Board of Control, the building was considered quite elegant when it opened, with a handsomely appointed practice courtroom and a law library, as well as offices and classrooms.

Today, the old west entrance with its arched opening at the base of a square tower with crenelated roofline faces the Emerson Courtyard, which links Bryan to Matherly Hall and the modern Business Building. Arched windows are set in the gabled parapets, and overhanging bracketed eaves are an unusual feature.

The original building was enlarged several times to its current L-shaped configuration during the more than fifty years that it served as the state's only state-supported law school.

Florida governors Reuben Askew and Lawton Chiles studied here, as did U.S. Congressmen Charles Bennett, Sam Gibbons, Spessard Holland,

Area 1

Business Building

Bryan Hall

and George Smathers. At one time a considerable percentage of the Florida legislature took its early legal training in the law libraries and moot courts of Bryan Hall. Today, Florida's future business leaders are trained here, with such modern resources as the Media Viewing Room. The offices of the Dean of the Warrington College of Business Administration, the MBA program, and the Department of Marketing are also located in Bryan Hall.

Bas-relief decorations of law book and gavel, the scale of justice, and other legal symbols in a variety of styles embellish Bryan Hall.

12. Matherly Hall
University Avenue

The four-story Warrington College of Business Administration building was named for Walter Jeffries Matherly, dean of the college from 1926 to 1954. Board of Control architect Guy Fulton designed Matherly in the early 1950s, principally for use as a classroom building.

Matherly Hall exemplifies the University's attitude toward strengthening the fabric of the campus through the use of materials that complement the Collegiate Gothic style of the early buildings. Horizontal bands of windows alternate with broad bands of brick, emphasizing the linear quality of the design. On the southwest corner, the main entrance to Matherly Hall is at the base of a four-story square tower block featuring a sandstone entablature and squared pilasters. A stylized bas-relief at the roofline, above a tall arched window, is the tower's only decoration.

Like Bryan Hall and the Business Building, Matherly Hall faces toward the Emerson Courtyard, the open-air forum and gathering place for the Warrington College of Business Administration, renamed in 1996 in honor of Alfred Warrington, a 1958 UF graduate who has been a generous and committed benefactor for many years.

Matherly Hall

13. Anderson Hall
University Avenue

Originally called Language Hall, this Collegiate Gothic building was constructed as a multiple purpose building. When it was completed in 1913, it provided classroom and office space for the English, history, classics, languages, and mathematics departments, and also administrative offices for the president, the registrar, and the Graduate School. The four-story red brick building also had space for student extracurricular activities, and housed the university's early literary and debating societies. Florida Blue Key was organized here and held its first meeting in President Murphree's office.

This distinguished building was designed by William A. Edwards, who became the official architect of the Board of Control and designed all of the campus buildings built before 1925.

Anderson Hall

In 1949, Language Hall was renamed for Dr. James Nesbitt Anderson, a professor of Latin and Greek who had been on the faculty of the Florida Agricultural College in Lake City, one of UF's forerunners. He was the first Dean of the College of Arts and Sciences and first Dean of the Graduate School.

Anderson Hall helps set the architectural tone to those passing the campus on University Avenue. Its principal entrance, facing north, was oriented to face University Avenue and the growing city of Gainesville, indicating the early founders' intention not to isolate the new university, but to integrate it into the surrounding community. Anderson Hall is undergoing restoration, including its original grand entrances, and renovations that will take it gracefully into the twenty-first century.

14. Smathers Library

The completion of the new library building in 1926 filled a pressing need. It also represented a major commitment to collecting the scholarly books and other printed materials that are essential to a true university. The Smathers collection includes rare books and manuscripts and collections devoted to Florida history, theatre, children's literature, Latin America, and Judaica; and the papers of well-known authors, such as Zora Neale Hurston and Marjorie Kinnan Rawlings.

The last building designed by architect William A. Edwards—Library East, as it came to be called—retained its interior and exterior Gothic features and ornamentation through major additions in 1931 and 1949. The brick building has a red tile roof, parapets, capped buttresses, a square tower, and terra cotta embellishments. On the interior are wood-beamed and coffered ceilings, stone archways, carved oak paneling, and recessed Gothic archways encasing lancet windows.

After the last expansion, in the early 1950s artist Hollis Holbrook painted a dramatic egg tempera mural, "The History of Learning in Florida," on one wall of the grand Humanities Reading Room in the south wing. It depicts the tree of life and figures of Florida authors, governors, and other historical images.

George Smathers, U.S. Senator from 1951 to 1969, and a former UF student body president (1937–38), made a significant donation to the libraries, which were renamed in his honor in 1991.

Area 1

Smathers Library

Library West

15. Library West
University Avenue and Newell Drive

The north end of the Plaza of the Americas is bounded by Library West, which opened in 1967 principally as a research library for graduate students. Books that had been packed away for lack of shelf space found a home at last. There was now room for the rare books and manuscript collection, the P.K. Yonge Library of Florida History, and the Belnap Collection for the Performing Arts. The heroic bronze statue by Henry Moore, called "The Archer," was acquired to celebrate this major expansion of the university's library system and is still displayed in the main lobby.

Library West currently houses the humanities collection, the official U.S. documents collection, the microform collection of periodicals and records, and a large array of reference materials. Following a major renovation in the early 1990s, the special collections were moved to the adjacent Smathers Library (Library East) to make room for the expanding number of books, periodicals, and research materials, as well as the computers used to search for and locate the library's holdings.

The five-story brick structure has a red tile roof and is linked to the adjacent Smathers Library by a covered walkway.

16. Plaza of the Americas
Newell Drive and Union Road

Although the broad quadrangle between the University Auditorium and Library West was a part of the 1906 campus plan, it did not receive its formal title until 1931, when trees were planted to mark the first meeting of the Institute of Inter-American Affairs. University of Florida President John J. Tigert had invited representatives of the nations of the Americas to meet on campus in a four-day session which was intended to foster better relations among the countries of the two hemispheres. In honor of this occasion, twenty-one trees, each labeled with the name of a specific country, were planted with due ceremony.

The Plaza of the Americas serves as the University's open-air forum, a place where politics, religion, morals, and manners are hotly debated beneath the stately oaks and magnolia trees.

For more than twenty years the Hare Krishna community of Alachua County has brought food to the Plaza each day classes are held, accepting

Area 1

Plaza of the Americas

only voluntary donations from those who line up for a heaping plate of vegetarian fare. They served their one millionth meal in November of 1996. Sometimes-rowdy holiday celebrations and protest rallies have drawn large crowds to this quadrangle, but on most days, it is a peaceful scene of students lounging under the shady trees, musicians strumming guitars, and pedestrians ambling along the sidewalks that criss-cross the Plaza's grassy lawn.

AREA 2

1. Turlington Hall
Newell Drive and Union Road

Although Turlington Hall is clad in red brick, its modern, asymmetrical plan is a radical departure from the earlier academic buildings on campus. With its porthole windows and prowlike upper story, it resembles a great ocean liner run aground in an oak forest. Occupying a prominent location just west of the University Auditorium and Century Tower, it was the largest classroom building on campus and became a pivotal social center for students who gather between classes in the plaza, around "The Rock," in the brick-enclosed spaces, along the walls, around tables set out by clubs and organizations, and in the arcade leading to the food-vending machines.

"The Rock," a thirty-thousand-year-old, ten-ton chunk of Florida chert, was donated by a phosphate company to the Department of Geology and installed in front of the building in 1984.

First called General Purpose Building A, or GPA, Turlington Hall was renamed for Gainesville native and UF graduate Ralph Turlington, a member of the state legislature for twenty-four years and later the Florida Commissioner of Education. The Dean of the College of Liberal Arts and Sciences and the departments of Anthropology, Geology, English, History, Sociology, Political Science, and Geography are headquartered in the four-story building.

Turlington has a bewildering maze of classrooms, including three large lecture halls on the south end, and a basement with more labs and offices. Tradition has it that there are still students wandering around Turlington Hall who should have graduated in the 1980s, looking for the classrooms where their final exams are to be held.

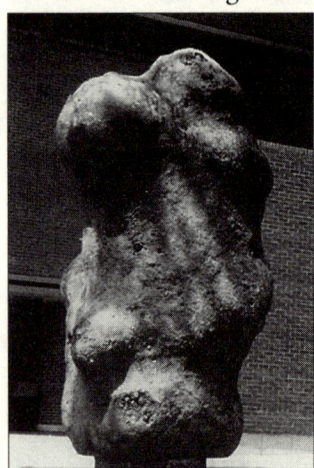

The rock

154

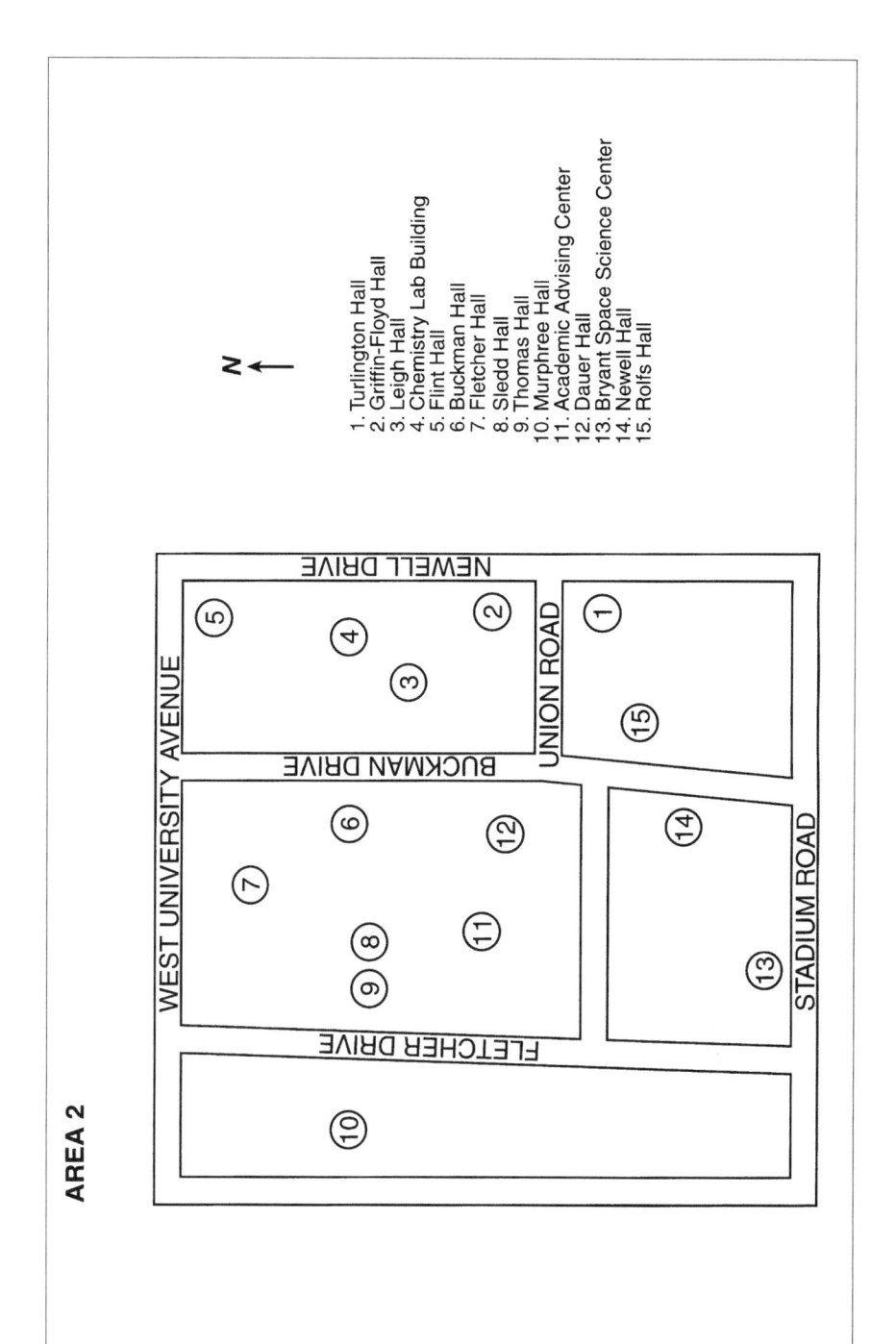

AREA 2

N ←

1. Turlington Hall
2. Griffin-Floyd Hall
3. Leigh Hall
4. Chemistry Lab Building
5. Flint Hall
6. Buckman Hall
7. Fletcher Hall
8. Sledd Hall
9. Thomas Hall
10. Murphree Hall
11. Academic Advising Center
12. Dauer Hall
13. Bryant Space Science Center
14. Newell Hall
15. Rolfs Hall

2. Griffin-Floyd Hall
Union Road and Newell Drive

A cornucopia full of fruit spills into an open basket in a terra cotta bas-relief above the east and north doors of Griffin-Floyd Hall. The sculpture represents the abundance of Florida's agricultural products, a fitting symbol for the first home of the College of Agriculture. Dairy cows were once led into the cattle judging arena on the first floor, while on the second floor, the general assembly hall served as a chapel where all the students attended daily religious exercises.

Completed in 1912, the building was named for Major Wilbur L. Floyd, professor of physics, biology, and horticulture, and assistant dean of the College of Agriculture from 1915 to 1938. Floyd served at both the University of Florida and at the East Florida Seminary in Gainesville, one of the five institutions amalgamated by the Buckman Act in 1905.

Boarded up for many years, and once slated for demolition, Floyd Hall was rescued by a generous $2 million gift of Ben Hill Griffin Jr., legendary

Floyd Hall in 1919
Florida State Archives

citrus pioneer and rancher, ardent UF benefactor, and a UF agriculture and business student in the 1930s. The sensitive and elegant renovation of the building was completed in 1992. The great central stairway was restored, and in the east foyer paintings honor fifteen faculty members who taught Ben Hill Griffin Jr. during his years at the University of Florida.

The departments of Philosophy and Statistics are now housed in Griffin-Floyd Hall.

3. Leigh Hall
Buckman Drive

The cornerstone of Leigh Hall was laid in 1926, when the building was dedicated as the Chemistry-Pharmacy Building. The first phase of the Collegiate Gothic building, designed by Rudolph Weaver, the newly appointed architect for the Board of Control, called for a hollow square design with an open courtyard in the center of the building.

Over time, other additions and improvements have been made to accommodate the fast-growing departments and their teaching and research activities. The Department of Chemistry pioneered graduate study at UF, awarding the first Ph.D. degree in 1934. The west wing, completed in 1949, provided badly needed space for the College of Pharmacy. Soon afterwards the building was renamed in honor of Dr. Townes R. Leigh, head

Leigh Hall

of the Department of Chemistry (1920–49) and a former dean of the College of Arts and Sciences and UF vice president. When the College of Pharmacy moved to new quarters in the J. Hillis Miller Health Center in 1962, the Department of Chemistry was left in full possession of the building.

On the facade of Leigh Hall, the names of famous scientists such as Boyle, Curie, Lavoisier, and Pasteur appear in raised stone lettering along the cornice. Whimsical gargoyles near the roofline represent the ancient arts of alchemy, and alchemical symbols for the elements are repeated in stone and on the copper rain gutters. A fine two-story oriel window is a distinctive feature of the east facade.

In 1965–66, the Chemistry Research Building was added to the south end of the complex, greatly expanding the department's modern laboratory facilities. In 1994 the university completed a $10 million renovation of Leigh Hall.

4. Chemistry Laboratory Building
Newell Drive

Work on the four-story Chemistry Laboratory Building (CLB) began in 1988 and continued into 1990. The multiple gables, tile roof, and stone surrounds on the square windows link the massive brick building to the Collegiate Gothic architectural tradition of the campus.

The CLB was deliberately located far enough north of adjacent Leigh Hall to save the large oak trees that shade the walkway between the two buildings and to preserve Leigh Hall's historic facade. The sculpture of brick clay on the wall outside the Chemistry Laboratory Building's state-of-the-art lecture hall, "Squares on Squares" by Charles J. Fager, casts interesting shadows and lends drama to the new building.

Most of the CLB is devoted to advanced research in analytical, inorganic, and physical chemistry. On the ground floor are machine shops where equipment is fabricated and maintained.

5. Flint Hall
University Avenue and Newell Drive

Science Hall was completed in 1910, and became the home of the departments of Botany, Chemistry, Horticulture, Physics, Zoology, and Bacteriology. The University Museum, which became the Florida State

Area 2

Symbol over door on Leigh Hall

Flint Hall

Museum in 1914 by act of the Florida Legislature, occupied the second floor. Professor Thompson Van Hyning was the curator of this natural and cultural history collection until his retirement in 1945.

Among the distinguished scientists who taught in the building was Dr. Edward R. Flint, professor of chemistry and also the university physician, for whom the hall is named.

The three-story red brick building forms a rectangle. Its roofline is crenelated in white terra cotta, a feature that it shares with Thomas, Buckman, and Newell Halls. Many of the other decorative terra cotta elements—as well as carved woodwork, Gothic vaulting, plasterwork, and formal stairways on the interior—were removed in the 1950s when the building was altered and designated for storage. The College of Liberal Arts and Sciences hopes to restore Flint Hall and return it to academic and scientific use once more.

6. Buckman Hall
Buckman Drive

Completed in 1907, but occupied by students when the University of Florida opened in the fall of 1906, Buckman Hall is the smaller of the two original campus buildings. Its Collegiate Gothic style evokes a feeling of solidity and permanence.

Like Thomas Hall, the other original building, Buckman was a multi-purpose facility with classrooms as well as dorm rooms. During World War I, soldiers lived in Buckman Hall and drilled on the lawn in front. The north wing of Buckman Hall was used for classrooms until after World War II, but it has been used exclusively as a residence hall since then.

The three-story brick building has a garret beneath its pitched, red-tile roof. Its gabled dormer windows are linked by a low crenelated wall. The six bays that project from the east facade and rise two stories are decorated with water spouts set into a floral design. Above each entrance is a plaque representing the Anguished

The Anguished Scholar

Area 2

Scholar, a somewhat frightening image for incoming students facing their first year of college life. The building is named for Henry Buckman, the legislative leader who authored the higher education consolidation bill that established the University of Florida in Gainesville.

7. Fletcher Hall
Buckman Drive

Fletcher Hall was built in 1939, late in the Depression and largely with federal funds, to alleviate a serious housing shortage on campus. Designed by Rudolph Weaver in the Collegiate Gothic style, the residence hall has many interesting and varied architectural details. Stone balustrades alternate with wall dormers at the roofline of the three-and-a-half-story building. An oriel window is set in the tower block above the north entrance leading to the inner courtyard. Oriel and bay windows with leaded glass and carved stone embellish each facade, and each entrance has a different design, creating a lively sampler of architectural styles. The seals of some of the world's great universities appear on the walls of Fletcher Hall, and charming birds and animal figures of carved stone are set in the door and window surrounds.

Fletcher Hall is connected on the south end to Sledd Hall. When seen from the air, the complex of dormitories formed by Buckman, Fletcher, Sledd, and Thomas Halls seem to form the letters UF.

The building, at first called North Hall, was named for U.S. Senator Duncan U. Fletcher, a staunch supporter of the University of Florida.

Renovated in 1984, Fletcher is now an air-conditioned, coed residence hall.

Figurines on Fletcher Hall

8. Sledd Hall
Fletcher Drive

Sledd Hall was named for the first UF president, Andrew Sledd (1905–09), who had been president of Florida Agricultural College in Lake City, a forerunner of the University of Florida. Sledd was an outstanding scholar in Latin and Greek, earning his doctorate from Yale University. He received the University of Florida's first honorary degree, Doctor of Divinity, in 1909 at the first UF commencement.

Sledd Hall, which was designed by Rudolph Weaver, was built in 1930 and dedicated in 1939. The three-and-a-half-story dormitory is irregularly shaped, and is linked to Fletcher and Thomas Halls. Two-story bay windows have balconies at the third-story level that are embellished with seals of the world's great universities, for example, Yale, Harvard, and the universities of Prague, Vienna, Upsala, and Heidelberg. Carved stone animals, plants, and figures are set in the springlines above deeply recessed vestibules; gargoyles along the cornice line depict students in various activities; and a brick wall with stone coping and square pillars connects Sledd to Buckman Hall on the east, enclosing an inner courtyard.

Sledd Hall

Sledd Hall's most distinctive feature is the Mucozo Tower on the south facade. Designed by UF art professor W.K. Long, the entry is carved with symbols of Florida's Indian and Spanish heritage. It is named for Chief Mucozo, who befriended one of the first Spaniards to land in Florida, Juan Ortiz, whose image is also carved on the tower's facade. A passageway through the tower leads to another inner courtyard, often used by the residents for volleyball games and other informal activities.

9. Thomas Hall
Fletcher Drive

Named for Gainesville Mayor William R. Thomas, a key figure in bringing the University of Florida to the city, Thomas Hall was completed in 1906. It was the first of the two original multipurpose buildings designed by the architectural firm of Edwards and Walters. William A. Edwards of this firm designed all of the campus buildings until the mid-1920s.

The long central section of Thomas Hall is oriented north and south with short end wings that run east and west. Each facade has two-story bays with balconies inset with decorative stone drains. A small bas-relief of youngsters reading and playing adorns the wall surface above the east entrance. Thomas is connected to Sledd Hall and forms one side of the oak-shaded enclosed courtyard of the dormitory complex.

Thomas Hall originally contained the president's office, classrooms, library, dining hall and kitchen, a four-bed infirmary, and a small auditorium. It became a residence hall as other facilities were built on campus. Renovations through the years have improved the facilities without compromising the historic exterior of this venerable structure.

10. Murphree Hall
University Avenue and Fletcher Drive

Named for UF's second president, Alfred A. Murphree, this C-shaped red brick building, completed in 1939, was one of the last buildings to be designed by Board of Control architect Rudolph Weaver in the traditional Collegiate Gothic style. The three-and-a-half-story building is located west of the older residence halls. It was built during the Depression with federal assistance.

UNIVERSITY OF FLORIDA

The Mucozo Tower archway, Sledd Hall

Area 2

Murphree Hall's distinguishing architectural features are the recessed arched entryways, the two-story bay windows with balconies on the third floor, and shed dormers set in the red tile roof.

For several years after World War II, families of veterans who were enrolled at UF on the GI Bill were housed here; diapers and baby buggies replaced pennants and pin-ups as the young families balanced study hours and homemaking in the dorm. After that brief era, the football team was quartered here for a time. Murphree is still a residence hall for undergraduates, one of the complex of five original dorms that are included in the University of Florida's historic district, listed on the National Register of Historic Places in 1989.

Murphree Hall

11. Academic Advising Center
Fletcher Drive

The University Athletic Association contributed half the cost of the new Academic Advising Center, which serves thousands of undergraduate students and student athletes each semester. The center houses tutoring rooms, study halls, and computer and audio/visual labs for student athletes and also the offices of advisors and administrators.

A handsome impressionistic painting by artist Heidi Edwards strikes the eye of the visitor upon entering the main lobby. The thirty-thousand-square-foot building was designed with some features of the predominant Collegiate Gothic style of the older buildings on campus, such as bay windows and gables at the roofline.

The center occupies the site of Johnson Hall, the original UF Commons, or dining hall and rathskeller, built in 1912 and destroyed by fire in December 1987.

12. Dauer Hall
Union Road and Buckman Drive

Dauer Hall was built during the Depression as the Florida Union, a multi-purpose center of student life, with a soda fountain in the basement, lounges on the first floor, an auditorium/chapel and classrooms on the second floor, and office space for student government and organizations on the third floor. Its first director was D.R. "Billy" Matthews, who later served in the U.S. Congress.

For several years, the student newspaper, *The Florida Alligator*, shared space in the basement with the bookstore and the game room. In 1967, the Florida Union relocated to the J. Wayne Reitz Union, and the building was turned over to the College of Liberal Arts and Sciences for classrooms and faculty offices. The building was renamed for Professor Manning Dauer, chair of the Department of Political Science from 1950 to 1975.

Bas-relief on Dauer Hall

Area 2

Academic Advising Center

The huge windows with Gothic tracery on the north and south facades of the west wing illuminate the grand banquet room with its beamed ceiling, later converted to a language lab. On the east facade, light from the stunning stained glass window reflecting universal spiritual beliefs with a Florida motif floods the former chapel on the second floor, named in honor of Ruth McQuown, associate dean of the College of Liberal Arts and Sciences. The southeast entrance vestibule is decorated with a whimsical fresco of birds and squirrels perched on branches of orange trees. Over the northwest entrance, to the rear of the building, is a fine bas-relief of a youth playing a lute. Such graceful details appear on all the historic campus buildings, even those built in the depths of the Depression.

13. Bryant Space Science Center
Stadium Road

Resembling a modern fortress with narrow slits of windows and expanses of unbroken brick walls, Bryant Space Science Center was dedicated in June of 1968. Originally designated as the Space Center Research Building, it was later named for Thomas Bryant, a member of the Board of Control.

Bryant Space Science Center

Area 2

The five-story building with its adjacent computer wing was largely funded by a $1.2 million NASA grant to accommodate a range of interdisciplinary studies related to the exploration of outer space. As a graduate teaching center, it was equipped with a powerful IBM 236D computer, mass spectrometer, a "floating room" to study sleep problems in space, and other specialized equipment. It now houses the Department of Astronomy, the Laser Science Lab, and the Northeast Regional Data Center (NERDC).

14. Newell Hall
Buckman Drive

Built as the Florida Agricultural Experiment Station in 1910, Newell Hall represents the close link between the academic mission of the University and practical agricultural services to the growers and farmers of the state. Founded with federal funds in 1888 at the Florida Agricultural College, a land grant college located in Lake City, the Experiment Station moved to the Gainesville campus when the University of Florida was established in 1905. It operated from Thomas Hall until this building was completed. Extensive botanical and horticultural gardens and experimental fields were laid out on adjacent grounds, and students received hands-on research experience.

Newell Hall

The building's name honors Dr. Wilmon E. Newell, Director of the Agricultural Experiment Station and Provost for Agriculture. A noted entomologist, Newell took an active role in protecting Florida's citrus crops from the Mediterranean fruit fly.

Newell Hall resembles the early collection of Collegiate Gothic buildings with its roof clad in red tiles, accented by dormers and a crenelated parapet. It was originally built of brick over a wood frame, but in 1943 the interior was gutted and a steel-and-concrete frame inserted inside the brick shell. Arched above the east entry is a wrought-iron sign identifying Newell Hall, which is now occupied by the departments of Soil and Water Science, and Agronomy.

15. Rolfs Hall
Buckman Drive

The Horticulture Building was designed to meet the growing needs of UF's agricultural programs. Completed in 1927, it housed the Agricultural Extension Service, the State Plant Board, and the Agricultural Experiment Station, as well as classrooms. Here, too, the UF Herbarium, a comprehensive collection of dried and preserved plant materials from all over the world, was established to assist in plant study and identification.

The building was renamed in the 1950s for Professor Peter Henry Rolfs, Dean of the College of Agriculture and Director of the Agricultural Experiment Station. The Florida oak, *Quercus rolfii*, was also named for this distinguished horticulturist.

The red brick building was to have additions to the east and south, but these were never completed. The parapet that links the roof dormers is pierced with quatrefoils and lozenges, and a wreathed beehive plaque set in the south bay of the west parapet honors the horticulturalist's natural ally.

Although Rolfs Hall is dominated on the east by the adjacent mass of Turlington Hall, its west facade presents a graceful counterpoint to Newell Hall across the street.

Rolfs Hall is now the home of the innovative IBM computer network writing lab and the Center for Teaching Excellence.

AREA 3

1. Florida Gymnasium
Stadium Road

Cheering fans roared their approval of each basket scored in Alligator Alley, the nickname of the basketball court in the Florida Gym. The men's varsity team played here for thirty-one seasons, from 1949 until the O'Connell Center opened. The last SEC contest in February of 1980 pitted the Gators against Vanderbilt, after which the Stephen O'Connell Center became the home of the UF hoopmen.

Usually packed to the rafters, the often hot and always noisy indoor stadium also hosted big-name performers such as Bob Hope. Peter, Paul, and Mary and Ray Charles set the rafters ringing when the Florida Gym was used for concerts during its heyday. For decades, students stood in lines all around the court to register for classes each semester. Blue Key banquets

Florida Gym in 1960
Florida State Archives

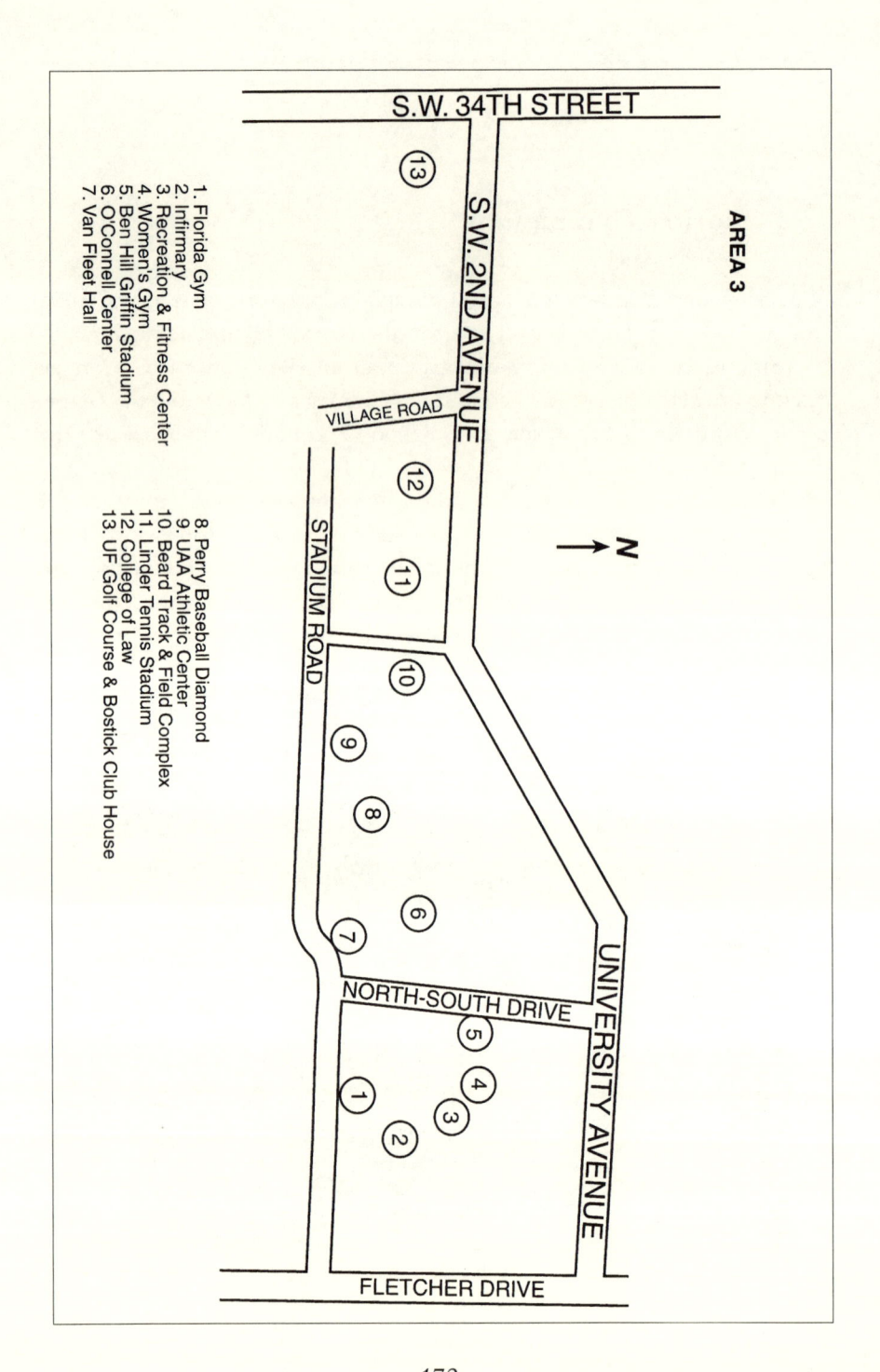

AREA 3

1. Florida Gym
2. Infirmary
3. Recreation & Fitness Center
4. Women's Gym
5. Ben Hill Griffin Stadium
6. O'Connell Center
7. Van Fleet Hall
8. Perry Baseball Diamond
9. UAA Athletic Center
10. Beard Track & Field Complex
11. Linder Tennis Stadium
12. College of Law
13. UF Golf Course & Bostick Club House

Area 3

were also held here, drawing political speakers such as John F. Kennedy, Richard Nixon, and Lyndon Johnson, as well as governors, cabinet members, and other top government officials.

The symmetrical main facade is dominated by the central bay, framed by stone-capped buttresses, and the broad arch of the main entrance. The basketball arena has a separate curved roof. The red brick building was recently renovated to make it accessible to all students. Classrooms and offices of the College of Health and Human Performance, headquartered in the Florida Gym, have also been remodeled. The basketball court continues to be used for intramural basketball contests.

2. **Infirmary**
Fletcher Drive

Small carved stone figures—one grasping a crutch, one holding a huge saw, one measuring out medicine, and one suffering, perhaps from homesickness—peer down on students checking into the Student Health Center, or Infirmary, for treatment of aches and pains, measles shots, and other medical needs.

Before 1931, when the brick Collegiate Gothic building opened, students were treated in a recycled World War I barracks building. The state-of-the-art new Infirmary included an operating room and beds for ailing students and functioned like a small hospital. When Shands Hospital was built, the Infirmary's role changed. Since 1983 it has been an outpatient clinic. A residence for nurses was added on to the original building at the south end in 1947, and the pharmacy was added in the rear in 1975. The interior has recently been completely renovated, streamlining service to the students whose fees support the facility.

3. **Student Recreation and Fitness Center**
Fletcher Drive

Just to the east of the Ben Hill Griffin Stadium is the Student Recreation and Fitness Center, adjoining the Florida Gym and the outdoor swimming pool.

In front, on the east side, is the light-flooded Racquet Club restaurant, architecturally a complementary blend of the Collegiate Gothic and contemporary styles. Like most of the newer buildings on campus, this structure has original art as part of the interior design, in this case a series of

UNIVERSITY OF FLORIDA

Infirmary

Student Recreation and Fitness Center

bright, up-beat paintings of Florida images by artist John Walton, located in the dining area. A small convenience store, handy for students living in the nearby dorms, is tucked into the north corner.

Behind the dining facility is the Fitness Center, which houses eight racquetball courts, two squash courts, a volleyball and basketball court, two aerobic dance rooms, a strength and conditioning room, and Lifestyle Appraisal Center. The Lifestyle Appraisal Center, which has been open since 1991, provides members with a personal fitness profile and computerized dietary analysis, and incentives such as a walking club and "the Stadium Stompers," a group that meets regularly to keep in shape by climbing up and down the bleachers of the nearby stadium. Like the Southwest Recreation Park and the UF Recreational Sports Program, this center is administered by the College of Health and Human Performance.

4. Women's Gymnasium
Fletcher Drive

Big-league baseball came to Gainesville in 1918, and as part of the process, the City of Gainesville chipped in to finish the new University of Florida gymnasium. President Murphree had invited John McGraw, the manager of the New York Giants, to hold his team's spring training on the campus, and the city council was so excited that they voted to donate $1,000 to put finishing touches on the new red brick building to accommodate the team. The Giants played the University of Florida baseball team in March, drawing a crowd of about a thousand and beating the college team by only eight runs. In April, exhibition games between the Giants and the Boston Red Sox attracted some three thousand fans to Fleming Field.

Referred to today as the Women's Gym, the brick and stone building has a facade of high segmented windows set within the buttressing wings of the central arch. The building has been used for basketball games, and served as well as an auditorium, movie theater, chapel, and social hall. The gymnasium was described by *The Florida Alligator* as "impressive in its grandeur," its interior flooded with light from the arched windows on all sides and the clerestory windows near the roof. From the gallery extending around the whole room, spectators could observe the floor of the court, whether a basketball game, a gymnastic meet, or a formal dance was in progress. In 1930, the outdoor swimming pool was added to the west of the building. When UF went coed in 1947–48, the building was turned over to women students for their athletic programs.

UNIVERSITY OF FLORIDA

5. Ben Hill Griffin Stadium at Florida Field
University Avenue and North-South Road

Crowds pour into the bowl-shaped football stadium on fall afternoons to cheer the Florida Gators on to victory, just as they have since 1930, when Florida Field saw its first Homecoming game. As the number of avid fans grew, the twenty-two-thousand-seat stadium was expanded time and again, until now eighty-three thousand fans may fill every available seat, from aluminum bleachers, to orange Quarterback Club armchairs, to air-conditioned "gator dens," to sumptuous skyboxes seven stories above the bright green grass field.

To honor his generous contributions to the athletic program, the facility was renamed for citrus magnate Ben Hill Griffin Jr. after the $17 million expansion in 1990. This added the glass bell-jar entrance, the Touchdown Terrace, and curving ramps leading up to new seats on the north end.

Beneath the south seats are the weight training rooms for the athletes, corridors lined with photos of UF athletic heroes, and the varsity football team locker rooms. Here, too, is the mythical Bull Gator statue poised just inside the home team's entrance to the field. Each UF player touches it for good luck as he runs out onto the field, The Swamp, to face the cheering crowds. The alligator has been the emblem of the UF team since 1908. It is said that all good Gators bleed orange and blue, the team colors.

Ben Hill Griffin Stadium

Area 3

Another tradition is the ringing of the Victory Bell, which was given to UF in 1950 when the USS *Florida* was decommissioned. A bronze plaque listing UF casualties in World War I, placed at Florida Field when the stadium was dedicated to those who had served in that war, was reinstalled on the ground floor of the new entrance that replaced the original red brick north wall of Florida Field.

6. **Stephen C. O'Connell Student Activity Center**
Stadium Road and North-South Drive

Unlike any other building on campus, or for that matter any other building in this part of the state, the O'Connell Center is partially constructed of space-age polymers, a waterproof fabric with a pressurized air system to keep it inflated.

Concrete beams and arches support the translucent fabric that covers the octagonal building, located in the center of the campus sports complex. Live plants and trees grow on the earthen berms inside the O'Dome, thriving in the sunlight filtering through the ceiling and the comfortable climate-controlled temperature within the structure.

Named for the sixth president of the university, the Stephen C. O'Connell Center honors a man who was a talented athlete (a star boxer) and campus leader during his days as a UF student (1934–40) and who later served on the Florida Supreme Court (1955–67). He was chief justice of

Stephen C. O'Connell Center

the Court in 1967 when he accepted the presidency of the University. O'Connell was the first UF alumnus and the first Florida native to become president of the University of Florida.

Opened in 1981, the Center can seat twelve thousand spectators and accommodate one thousand persons participating in eight separate physical activities simultaneously. The O'Connell Center is the scene of graduations, concerts, basketball games, gymnastic meets, swimming and diving competitions, exhibitions, banquets, and countless other events.

7. **Van Fleet Hall**
Stadium Road

Major James A. Van Fleet was commandant of the Army ROTC and a professor of military science and tactics at the University of Florida in the 1920s. He also coached the UF varsity football team to outstanding seasons in 1923 and 1924. He returned to the Army to continue his military career, and, during World War II, having attained the rank of general, commanded the U.S. Eighth Army and also the United Nations ground forces during the Korean conflict. General Van Fleet received an honorary degree from the University of Florida, and the building, constructed in 1952 for the ROTC, was named in his honor.

The three-story brick building is now headquarters for four branches of the Reserve Officers Training Corps: the Navy and Marines man the bridge on the first floor, the Army is in command of the second level, and the top floor is the High Frontier of the Air Force ROTC. Intense pride in their service units is evident in the trophies, framed pictures, and military memorabilia displayed in the hallways of each floor.

Before the adjacent O'Connell Center was built, the cadets had a large parade ground to the north of their building. Several magnolia trees planted in front of Van Fleet Hall commemorate fallen servicemen who once served in the University of Florida ROTC units.

8. **Carl Perry Baseball Diamond and McKethan Stadium**
Stadium Road

Baseball is a proud tradition at the University of Florida, with over eighty seasons of play. UF Gators have won the coveted SEC title seven times, and thirty-five players have gone on to play for major league teams.

Area 3

Van Fleet Hall

Carl Perry Baseball Diamond and McKethan Stadium

The 4,500-seat stadium, named for Alfred A. McKethan—banker, civic leader, major contributor, and ardent baseball fan—was refurbished in 1988 with new seating. In 1995, a new press box was added and the main entrance redesigned. Bull Gator booster George Steinbrenner, principal owner of the New York Yankees, donated the lights. First installed in 1977, these lights do double duty, providing handy nesting sites for several families of ospreys.

The actual playing field, which has natural grass and a red clay playing surface, is named for Carl "Tootie" Perry, captain of the 1921 varsity football game. Perry, a Gainesville businessman, was known as the "All-American Waterboy," enthusiastically volunteering as the Gator team's waterboy for many seasons at Florida Field.

9. University Athletic Association Athletic Center
Stadium Road

Located between the Beard Track and Field Complex and the Perry Baseball Field is a new facility for varsity athletes. Opened in 1995, it is the home of the UF women's volleyball team, which uses the three-court gymnasium for practice. There are also offices and locker rooms for the men's and women's track teams and the women's baseball, soccer, and volleyball teams. Athletic trainers tend to the needs of UF's varsity athletes in the well-equipped training and sports medicine area.

Skylights set in the flat roof of the brick building admit natural light. Above the front entrance hangs a mobile composed of silhouettes of women athletes engaged in a wide variety of sports, signifying the commitment of the UF athletic program to its women athletes for over twenty-five years. During this time, UF's women's teams have won twelve national titles and seven SEC All-Sports trophies. Individuals have won over one hundred national titles and 238 All-American rankings; thirty-nine UF women have competed in the Olympics, winning twenty-four medals, fourteen of them gold.

10. Percy Beard Track and Field Complex
Stadium Road and Southwest 2nd Avenue

Named for Percy Beard, UF track and field coach (1937–63) and former Olympic star, this superb outdoor complex is recognized as one of the finest collegiate track and field facilities in the country. The surface of the

Area 3

University Athletic Association Athletic Center

Percy Beard Track and Field Complex

nine-lane, 400-meter track is built to Olympic standards, patterned after that used in the 1984 Summer Olympics in Los Angeles. Fans sitting in the expanded grandstand not only have an excellent view of the oval track, but also of the other features—the multiple-jump runways, a steeplechase water jump, three circles for shot-put and discus, three high-jump approaches, and nine pole vault boxes.

Because of the superior quality of the complex and Gainesville's ideal year-round weather conditions, the Beard is used as a training facility not only by UF athletes, but also by many Olympic athletes, some of whom went on to win medals at the 1996 Olympics in Atlanta.

In addition to the outdoor facilities, UF also has an excellent 200-meter indoor track inside the Stephen C. O'Connell Center, reported to be one of the fastest tracks in the world for long sprints.

11. Scott Linder Tennis Stadium and Ring Tennis Pavilion
Southwest 2nd Avenue

The UF varsity tennis teams use the six lighted courts of the R. Scott Linder Tennis Stadium to defend team and individual honors. These honors are proudly displayed on bronze plaques on one of the brick walls in the complex, a recent one noting Jill Craybas's 1996 NCAA women's singles title.

The stadium, which opened in 1987, is named for UF alum, business leader, and major contributor R. Scott Linder. It is one of the premier tennis facilities in the region and can be used for year-round team training and practice, rain or shine.

In addition to the six stadium courts, there are six additional outdoor practice courts and three more courts within the Ring Tennis Pavilion. The covered pavilion, completed in 1996, was a gift of Alfred A. Ring, Gainesville philanthropist, tennis enthusiast, and professor emeritus of business administration.

12. College of Law
Southwest 2nd Avenue and Village Drive

Named for former Florida governor and U.S. Senator Spessard L. Holland, Holland Hall was the first building to be constructed in the University of Florida's new College of Law campus when the college moved from very

Area 3

Ring Tennis Pavilion

College of Law

overcrowded quarters in Bryan Hall in 1968. It was dedicated a year later by Chief Justice Earl Warren.

Located west of the main campus on a wooded site, the college's modern buildings contain classrooms, courtrooms, offices, and one of the finest college law libraries in the country. Holland Hall, which contains the Legal Information Center, is constructed of brick and concrete aggregate with fortresslike slit windows.

To its south is the two-story Bruton-Geer Hall, dedicated in 1984 and named for the parents of Judge and Mrs. James D. Bruton Jr. of Plant City, significant benefactors of the College of Law.

A tubular pedestrian walkway connects Holland and Bruton-Geer on the second floor, and an open patio with tree-shaded tables and benches provides an open-air forum for law students and faculty. Artist Stephen C. Oakley's intriguing sculpture in wood and copper, "Cause and Effect," is the dominant feature of this space between the two buildings.

The College of Law also has its own Indian mound, discovered when the site was being prepared. The mound was subsequently preserved and its presence noted by a historic marker on the corner of Southwest 2nd Avenue and Village Drive.

13. University Golf Course and Bostick Club House
Southwest 2nd Avenue and Southwest 34th Street

Originally laid out as the Gainesville Golf and Country Club, the eighteen-hole golf course anchors the far northwest corner of the main campus. UF acquired the course in 1962 and has developed an active program for both men's and women's golf, fielding varsity teams in college tournaments. Throughout the year, the course plays host to championship tournaments, including the Gator and Lady Gator Invitational and the Gator Golf Day Pro-Am, which matches alumni and current PGA tour players. Dozens of UF golfers have gone on to play the PGA tour, and Gator golfers have earned more than sixty All-American honors.

The Guy Bostick Club House, built in 1988, honors a UF alumnus and longtime booster of UF's golf program.

Area 3

University Golf Course

AREA 4

1. Fine Arts Complex
Southwest 13th Street and Stadium Road

The dramatic abstract sculpture fountain on Southwest 13th Street by former UF art faculty member Geoffrey Naylor sets off a complex of buildings built in the late 1960s for the College of Architecture and Fine Arts.

When the College of Architecture, which separated from Fine Arts in 1975, moved into its new buildings in 1978, the College of Fine Arts remained in the contemporary-style buildings, adding another structure for art studios and faculty offices. The University Gallery faces a small lecture hall across a sunken atrium. A four-story classroom building, which includes the College of Fine Art's Focus Gallery and the Marshall E. Rinker School of Building Construction, is linked to Rudolph Weaver Hall (named for the first director of School of Architecture) by an enclosed elevated walkway. The College of Fine Arts administrative offices, the Architecture and Fine Arts Library, and the Visual Resource Center (a vast collection of slides) are housed in this building.

Art students often take advantage of the open plaza surrounded by these buildings, or the tree-fringed ponds to the south and the west, to set up installations and open-air art projects. Some of these remain in place for years.

2. Architecture Building
Stadium Road

The dramatic curve of the glass-walled studio wing that forms the north facade of the College of Architecture building balances on tall concrete piers above an atrium. Architecture classes often gather in this atrium to critique building models and project drawings. Studios on the opposite side of the building have balconies and louvers to break the force of the southern sun. Broad open stairways angle to the side and zigzag up and down, and circular cutouts in the concrete create dramatic shade patterns. Overhead, the deliberately exposed pipes and tubes of the mechanical sys-

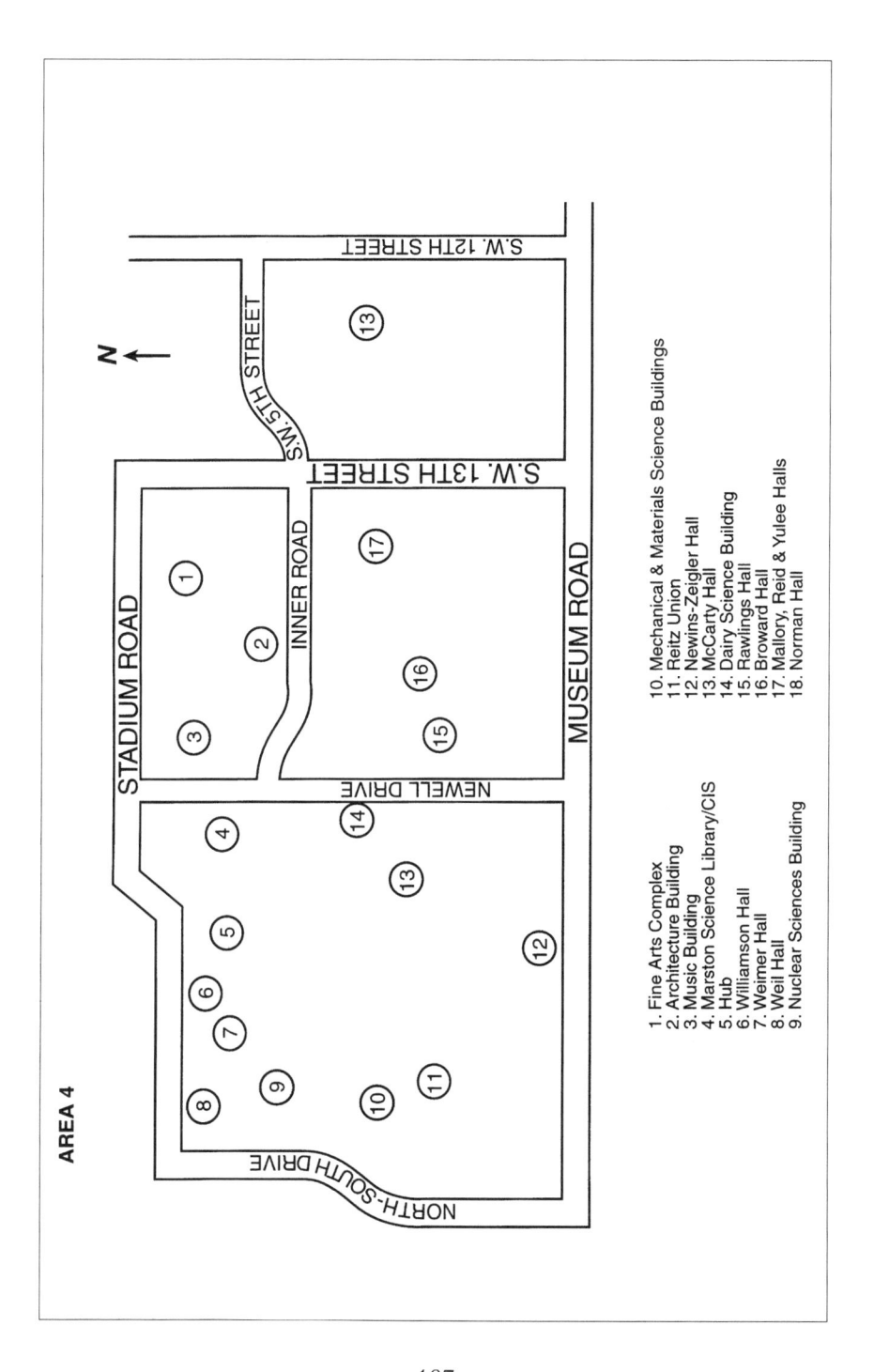

AREA 4

1. Fine Arts Complex
2. Architecture Building
3. Music Building
4. Marston Science Library/CIS
5. Hub
6. Williamson Hall
7. Weimer Hall
8. Weil Hall
9. Nuclear Sciences Building
10. Mechanical & Materials Science Buildings
11. Reitz Union
12. Newins-Zeigler Hall
13. McCarty Hall
14. Dairy Science Building
15. Rawlings Hall
16. Broward Hall
17. Mallory, Reid & Yulee Halls
18. Norman Hall

UNIVERSITY OF FLORIDA

Fountain near the Fine Arts Complex

Architecture Building

tems add to the building's texture. Classrooms and a teaching gallery are located on the ground level, opening on to the atrium overlooking the broad north lawn.

Connected to this building to the east is the four-story office complex for the college, where the dean of the college and the faculty of the departments of Architecture, Interior Design, Landscape Architecture, and Urban and Regional Planning are headquartered. The School of Architecture, which originally included Fine Arts, was organized in 1925. Rudolph Weaver, the architect for the campus buildings built from the late 1920s until the 1940s, served as its first director.

Andrew Ferandino, a graduate of the UF College of Architecture, was the principal architect of this award-winning building, which blends a playful and creative spirit with a practical learning environment.

3. Music Building
Stadium Road and Newell Drive

Enter the heart of the Music Building, the central commons, and you will often hear the faint sounds of bagpipes, drum rolls, or soprano trills from the practice rooms and studios, or music spilling from the open balconies as students tune their instruments. Climb the stairs to the music library on the second floor, and a few bars of piano jazz stray out a half-open door. Even the architecture of the building has a rhythmic feel, with brick facades that wave in and out, and walls that form sounding boards wrapped around the open landscaped atrium.

Music Building

UNIVERSITY OF FLORIDA

Dedicated in 1972 with a festival that featured distinguished American composer Aaron Copland, the Music Building represented a major turning point in the University of Florida's commitment to the arts. Although the Men's Glee Club had been formed in 1907 and the Gator Band was organized in the 1920s, it was not until the 1940s that formal music classes were offered at UF.

The Department of Music is part of the College of Fine Arts. Its students and faculty perform in the adjacent University Auditorium and the Center for the Performing Arts, where they may attend master classes with visiting artists such as Harry Connick Jr. or the Beaux Arts Trio. Within the Music Building are computers for electronic composition, an electronic piano lab, and practice and recital rooms that allow privacy while studying and playing. Students and faculty also make music on the UF carillon atop the Century Tower, on the Anderson Memorial Organ in the Auditorium, and as part of symphonic, marching, and jazz bands, trios and ensembles, and choral groups.

4. Marston Science Library and Computer and Information Science Building
Stadium Road and Newell Drive

Two massive buildings opened in 1987 in the center of the campus: the Marston Science Library and the Computer and Information Science Building. They balance and complement each other, seeming to pivot on the elegantly shaped vertical space under the glass canopy that links them. Their facades of brick and glass incorporate bands of copper to emphasize the horizontal lines of the two structures. The opening in the central atrium frames the Century Tower from the southwest. When approached from the northeast, it reveals the massive yellow aluminum-beam sculpture, "Alachua," by John R. Henry. (This abstract work caught the campus by surprise when it was installed; some called it "The French Fries from Hell.") The arrangement of the two buildings provides generous outdoor plazas on each side, terraced and planted with native trees and shrubs.

Each building consists of four floors and a basement, but each uses its interior spaces differently. The east building, named for the seventh UF President, Robert Q. Marston, contains a large collection of books and journals devoted to the physical, earth, and life sciences, and engineering and agriculture; the Map and Imaging Library; many computers to provide

Area 4

Marston Science Library and Computer and Information Science Building

on-line database searches; and quiet places to read and study. The west building has computer labs with over two hundred terminals, offices, classrooms wired to the University's mainframe computer, and an auditorium on the lower level. Special labs in the computer center are dedicated to the study of artificial intelligence, high-speed mind and machine interaction, computer vision, and other related areas of research.

5. **The Hub**
Stadium Road

Reflecting the University's first break with the Collegiate Gothic style, the Hub was completed in 1950 and was named by students in a campus-wide contest. The modern style combines elements of Art Deco with a lighthearted blend of sweeping curves and jazzy angles. Pancoast and Associates of Miami designed the Hub with three elements: the rectangular central block, a pavilion with a curved facade projecting from the west end, and a one-story rounded element to the east. Corrugated glass panels and concrete columns, some faced with colored tiles, and a sinuous covered walkway that embraces the green space in front set this building apart from the academic buildings surrounding it.

The Hub

A soda fountain and movie theater once catered to post–World War II students, many of them veterans and their wives, and shared space with the campus barber shop, post office, and bookstore.

The bookstore still occupies most of the first floor, displaying every conceivable type of Gator gear from sweatshirts and shoestrings to backpacks and baby clothes, in addition to textbooks, reference manuals, and best sellers. Hungry students stop by the Food Court for tacos, frozen yogurt, burgers, and other fast foods, and crowds spill out of the circular dining area to the surrounding patios during rush hours.

The second floor houses the Technology Hub, which has the latest in computers, software, and electronic gadgetry.

The Hub is where Gators come to pick up their caps and gowns before graduation, to order class rings, to buy a valentine card or gift, or to browse among the endless displays of orange-and-blue paraphernalia.

6. Williamson Hall
Stadium Road

Tucked between the Hub and Weimer Hall is Williamson Hall, the current headquarters of the Physics Department. It is named for Robert C.

Area 4

Willliamson Hall

Williamson, chair of the department from 1930 to 1958.

Built in the early 1960s, the three-story, L-shaped building has strong horizontal lines, with bands of buff-colored concrete aggregate alternating with aluminum-framed window walls. A glass-walled entry and stairwell rise above the main roofline, and a cantilevered concrete awning shelters the entrance to the Bless Auditorium (named for physics professor Arthur Bless, who taught from 1927 until 1951) located at the north end of the building. Williamson Hall contains classrooms, offices, teaching and research laboratories, and fabrication shops.

Adjacent to the east side of the building is the Physics Department's microkelvin lab, built in the mid-1980s for research in the properties of condensed matter at ultra-low temperatures. Much of the research carried out by the Physics Department is in collaboration with other departments and other universities, and Williamson Hall has extensive computing facilities linking it to other institutions worldwide.

A large new physics building is under construction a short distance to the south at the intersection of North-South Drive and Museum Road, an indication of the continuing expansion of the research carried out by the faculty and graduate students in the Physics Department.

7. Weimer Hall
Stadium Road

After spending several decades in the building under the west end of the stadium, the College of Journalism and Communications moved into its new home north of the Reitz Union in 1980. It is named for Dr. Rae O. Weimer, its first dean and first director of the School of Journalism, which became the College of Journalism and Communications in 1968. At that time over twelve hundred students were enrolled in the college, learning how to write for and manage newspapers and magazines, operate radio and television studios, and prepare advertising and public relations campaigns. The college operates three radio stations and a Public Broadcasting Service TV channel, with students in front of and behind the microphones and cameras.

The centerpiece of the John S. and James L. Knight Courtyard in the building's glass-ceilinged atrium, a gift of the Knight Foundation, is Don Bartlett's sculpture, "Media's People." Other areas of the building are also named for major donors: the 250-seat Gannett Auditorium, the Allen H. Neuharth Library, and the Alvin G. Flanagan Telecommunications wing.

The new Flanagan wing honors the 1941 UF graduate and retired chief of the Gannett Broadcasting Group and also houses the Joseph L. Brechner Center for Freedom of Information, named for the president of WFTV–Channel 9 in Orlando and a strong advocate of the freedom of information movement. The abstract stained glass panel over the entrance, "Macromicrochip II," is by Jim Piercey, and the wall sculpture in the lobby is by Marcia Raff.

Many of the graduates of the college have become well-known figures in the world of journalism and the media: Walter "Red" Barber, renowned sportscaster; Otis Boggs, "The Voice of the Gators"; Pulitzer Prize–winning journalist H. G. "Buddy" Davis; TV news analyst Forrest Sawyer; and *Miami Herald* columnist and novelist Carl Hiaasen.

8. Weil Hall
Stadium Road and North-South Drive

Originally called the Engineering Industries Building, Weil Hall opened in the late 1940s. It greatly alleviated the post–World War II space shortage on campus, especially for the popular engineering programs. It eventually

Detail over the door of Weil Hall

replaced Benton Hall (demolished in 1966) as the headquarters for the College of Engineering and still houses the administrative offices of the College and the departments of Civil Engineering, Coastal and Oceanographic Engineering, and Industrial and Systems Engineering.

Designed by architect Guy Fulton, Weil Hall was one of the last buildings on campus to remain true to the traditional Collegiate Gothic architectural style. The towerlike main entrance is embellished with Gothic lettering, a shield, and floral bas-reliefs. As the College of Engineering grew at a tremendous rate in subsequent decades, more wings were added to the south of the building (Reed Hall and the Nuclear Sciences Building), and other buildings dedicated to various engineering departments were built on adjacent sites.

The building is named for Joseph Weil, dean of the College of Engineering from 1937 to 1963. Weil pioneered radio tracking of hurricanes, among other endeavors, and during his twenty-six years as dean, he developed one of the top engineering colleges in the country.

UNIVERSITY OF FLORIDA

9. Nuclear Sciences Building

Connected to the south end of Weil Hall, this four-story building, completed in the mid-1960s, is modern in style, with bands of windows separated by panels of concrete aggregate and shaded by concrete awnings on each level. In keeping with campus tradition, red brick forms a horizontal pattern below the window lines and at the ends of the building. The main entrance, at the southeast corner, is dominated by a facade of smoked glass panels and a concrete canopy suspended from molded concrete supports.

In 1965, the installation of the four-million-volt Van de Graaf accelerator weighing six tons and standing three stories high propelled the University of Florida into the Nuclear Age. Designed to facilitate the study of nuclear reactions, it was the only one of its kind in the South and only one of six in the nation. The Department of Nuclear and Radiological Engineering prepares students to work with nuclear power systems, as well as conducting research on the application and safe use of nuclear radiation in medicine, space, and industry.

10. Mechanical Engineering and Materials Science Buildings
North-South Drive

The departments of Mechanical Engineering and Materials Science and Engineering are housed in two parallel buildings located south of Weil Hall and west of the Reitz Union. Each provides laboratory and office space for faculty and graduate students, as well as extensive experimental and computational facilities, including access to the university-wide computer system. Within each modern building are state-of-the-art specialized instruments and apparatus that facilitate advanced research projects and enable the faculty to train new generations of scientists and engineers. Polymer processing, thermodynamics, semiconductor processing, ceramic technology, biomedical research, intelligent machines, and robotics are only a few of the broad targeted areas of investigation that are carried out in these two buildings.

The modular look of each three-story structure is emphasized by the exposed cast concrete girders that define each level and the placement of the open stairways. They are similar in design to the College of Engineering buildings south of the Reitz Union and were dedicated, as were those buildings, in 1970.

Area 4

Nuclear Sciences Building

Mechanical Engineering and Materials Science Buildings

UNIVERSITY OF FLORIDA

11. J. Wayne Reitz Union
Museum Road

At the dedication ceremony in 1967, retiring UF president J. Wayne Reitz was surprised and delighted when it was announced that the new student union would bear his name. The Reitz Union, which was the largest student union in the South when it opened, is the place to grab a bite to eat, go bowling, catch a movie, attend a concert, cash a check, play a game of pool, get a haircut, pick up a gift or a greeting card, search for career guidance, learn darkroom techniques or weaving, or relax with friends—a place to unwind and feel comfortable. The Reitz Union replaced the original Florida Union in what is now Dauer Hall and took over some of the original functions of the Hub.

In 1990, the second level of the colonnade linking the multistory activities complex to the adjacent Constans Theater (named for Philip Constans, chairman of the Speech Department and director for many years of the Florida Players, the UF drama group) was enclosed. Here Margaret Ross Tolbert's stunning, impressionistic painting "Little Nemo's Spring" sets the tone for the fourteen new meeting and conference rooms that are named for Florida rivers and trees. The gallery on the second floor showcases student art works. The Rion Ballroom, named for William Rion, the Reitz Union's first director, hosts concerts, banquets, and formal dances.

J. Wayne Reitz Union

Area 4

The recent addition to the west for the new, expanded Career Resource Center has created a convenient drive-up entry to the Reitz Union, its thirty-eight hotel rooms, and its conference facilities. The tree-circled pond on the east side has been home to many generations of ducks, and it provides a relaxing waterfront ambiance for the variety of eating and drinking spots tucked into the Reitz Union, from the donut and pizza take-outs, to the outdoor patio, to the spacious food court that replaced the old cafeteria. More formal dining is available in the Arredondo Room on the fourth floor, named for Don Fernando de la Maza Arredondo who in 1817 was granted, for his service to the king of Spain, land that is now part of Alachua County.

12. Newins-Ziegler Hall
Museum Road

A canopied breezeway, like the shaded space beneath a great oak tree, links the two solid brick-walled sections of Newins-Ziegler Hall. To the west is the School of Forest Resources and Conservation, and to the east is the Department of Wildlife Ecology and Conservation.

Square and rectangular concrete pillars sculpted like tree trunks with abstract wood-grain designs support the roof of the two-story open space, which has an understory of scattered benches and low plantings.

Newins-Ziegler Hall

A Y-shaped stairway branches upward to the second floor where classrooms, laboratories, and offices are located.

Constructed in 1977, the building honors Dr. Harold S. Newins, first director of the School of Forestry, and Dr. Edwin A. Ziegler, long-time professor of forest economics and finances. While the original focus of the School of Forestry was to enhance the economic benefits and exploitation of the state's forest resources, the current research emphasis is on the conservation and protection of ecological resources, not only in Florida, but in other parts of the world as well.

13. **McCarty Hall**

In the mid-1950s, the College of Agriculture moved from its original quarters in Floyd Hall into a new complex of modern buildings. Even though there are four structures (A, B, C, and D), together they form McCarty Hall, named for former governor Dan McCarty, a 1934 UF graduate who became a successful citrus grower and cattleman.

The reinforced concrete and red brick buildings are four and five stories high, with aluminum window walls and elevated walkways that link the buildings at the upper stories.

The Institute of Food and Agricultural Sciences (IFAS), organized in 1964, has offices here also. IFAS consolidated the College of Agriculture, the Florida Agricultural Experiment Stations, the Florida Cooperative Extension Service, and other related entities to fulfill the teaching, research, and extension mission of the University of Florida. Some of these components date back to 1884 when UF's predecessor, the Florida Agricultural College in Lake City, was designated as a land-grant institution.

With a combined faculty of over five hundred, IFAS facilities support basic and practical research for the people of Florida and the rest of the world. From the development of Gatorade, tastier tomatoes, and more nutritious peanuts to integrated pest management and raising healthier dairy cattle on Caribbean islands, IFAS scientists and faculty work on age-old problems of feeding the nations and perform cutting-edge research into the secrets of microbes and cells. The adjacent Food Science and Human Nutrition Building is part of this complex, as well as a new addition, the Aquatic Food Products Laboratory.

McCarty Hall

14. Dairy Science Building (Building 120)
Newell Drive

Designed by Rudolph Weaver and built in 1937 as the Dairy Science Building, the small brick structure is linked to the style of earlier buildings on campus by the Gothic arch of the central entry pavilion on the east facade. Stone medallions depicting products of dairy science once were set in the north and south ends of the central gable, one depicting a mother and child with a bottle of milk, and one a scene of butter being churned.

Constructed during the Depression decade of the 1930s with federal funds, the Dairy Science Building housed offices, classrooms, a cold-storage room, and seven laboratories. Its modern equipment enabled the University to offer courses in dairy science and gave students practical experience in making cheese, manufacturing ice cream, and pasteurizing milk. One of the goals of the department's research was to find satisfactory means of preserving the summer surplus of milk produced in the state.

The structure now houses the IFAS Computer Network and is called Building 120.

UNIVERSITY OF FLORIDA

Dairy Science Building

Rawlings Hall

Area 4

15. **Rawlings Hall**
Newell Drive

Named for Florida's adopted daughter and one of the state's most renowned writers, Marjorie Kinnan Rawlings, this residence hall honors the Pulitzer Prize–winning author of *The Yearling*. Rawlings made her home in nearby Cross Creek from 1928 until her death in 1953. She became part of the University of Florida's intellectual and literary life, and left her estate, her home, her library, and her manuscripts to UF when she died.

For a time, before it became a State Park, her Cross Creek Cracker house was used as a retreat for creative writers in the English Department.

Rawlings Hall, dedicated in 1962 as a women's dormitory, displays the architectural style of that time with severe horizontal lines, a flat roof, corrugated aluminum panels, and a curving cantilevered concrete awning marking the main, west entrance.

16. **Broward Hall**
Inner Road

Built in the early 1950s to accommodate 630 women students, Broward Hall is a modern residence hall constructed in the form of the letter X. The architectural form and materials used in UF's first women's dormitory complex (Yulee, Mallory, and Reid Halls) just to the east were repeated in Broward Hall. The core contains a small dining hall and recreation room on the lower ground level with a main lobby on the first floor. Four residential wings spread out from the center. The windows of the four-story dorm wings are shaded by flat concrete awnings, and the modern styling emphasizes strong horizontal lines. In keeping with campus tradition, the walls are red brick, and flat clay tiles cover the hip roofs.

When the hall opened, a miniature golf course was laid out nearby for the use of the Broward coeds. Now a swimming pool between the Yulee area and Broward Hall draws large crowds in the summer months, and the sunken lawn to the southeast, known as the Broward Beach, is a favorite tanning spot and gathering place on sunny days. Adjacent tennis courts and playing fields are extensions of the wide range of recreational facilities available to students.

The residence hall is named for Annie Douglas Broward, a prominent Jacksonville businesswoman and the wife of Florida Governor Napoleon B. Broward, who was in office when UF was founded in 1905.

UNIVERSITY OF FLORIDA

Broward Hall

17. **Mallory, Reid, and Yulee Halls**
Southwest 13th Street and Inner Road

Built in 1950 to accommodate the new phenomenon of women students (UF had gone coed in 1947), these three buildings are linked by a central core to form a Y. They were the first on campus designed in the modern style, free of any overtones of Gothic form or decoration. Although the four-story residence halls are contemporary in styling, Guy Fulton, the architect for the Board of Control, used the same materials as the other buildings on campus to continue the unifying look of clay roof tiles, red brick, and stone or concrete trim.

The Board of Control mandated the functional modern style for it was quicker to build and less expensive. The contemporary dorm complex expresses its function through volume, mass, scale, and simplified details, such as the panels of glass block at the stair-tower entrances and large casement windows shaded by concrete ledges that form permanent awnings. Lounges on each floor with comfortable furnishings, a terraced porch, and such amenities as a complete laundry room, shampoo room with hair dry-

Area 4

Broward-Yulee Hall Area swimming pool

ers, and sewing room were designed to make the coeds feel at home.

In the 1950s, parents were reassured to note that the girls' dorms were all built on the east side of the campus, close to the sorority houses, and half a campus away from the boys' dorms and fraternity houses.

The three "girls' dorms" were the first buildings on the UF campus to be named for women. Angela Mallory, wife of Steven M. Mallory, U.S. Senator from Florida and former Confederate Secretary of the Navy, was a civic and social leader in Washington, and Richmond, Virginia, the Confederate capital. Mary Martha Reid, wife of territorial governor Robert Reid, established a hospital in Richmond for Florida sick and wounded soldiers during the Civil War. Nancy Wycliff Yulee, from a prominent Kentucky family, was the wife of David Levy Yulee, pioneer Florida statesman and the first U.S. Senator from Florida.

18. **Norman Hall**
Southwest 13th Street and Southwest 5th Avenue

Norman Hall, built in the 1930s across Southwest 13th Street from the main campus, originally served as the P.K. Yonge Laboratory School for grades K through 12. It now houses the College of Education.

UNIVERSITY OF FLORIDA

Norman Hall

    The steep red tile roof with hipped dormers, and the detailing of arched entrances, bay windows, Gothic tracery and lettering, and decorative brickwork are similar to the Collegiate Gothic architecture of the other buildings on campus. Stone figures here, however, reflect the very young scholars for whom the building was prepared—squirrels and a teacher introducing a bird to a small child at the north wing entrance for kindergarten children, a row of children's heads above the main "clock" entrance, a girl reading a book, and a miniature football player by the west doorway. A monumental figure of a woman holding a book, and overlooking the tree-shaded lawn, is set at the roofline on the west facade. A freestanding gymnasium, now used for folk dancing and karate classes, was built to the south of the main building.

    P.K.Yonge School, which honors the long-time chairman of the Board of Control, provided an excellent education for over four hundred youngsters, as well as a laboratory for teachers-in-training and an educational research center. In 1958 the school moved to a new facility at 1080 Southwest 11th Street, and the building was renamed for Dean James W. Norman, who led the College of Education from 1920 until 1955. A modern library and additional offices and classrooms were added to the east of the original building in the 1970s.

AREA 5

1. Gator Corner Dining Center
Stadium Road and North-South Drive

Attractively sited on the corner opposite the stadium and across from the O'Connell Center, the new Gator Corner serves all-you-can-eat meals to student athletes and other students who participate in the University's pre-paid meal plan. The gabled entrance vestibule leads into a spacious cafeteria area lined with sparkling blue, green, and white tile, and the dining areas seat 450.

Gator Corner Dining Hall

2. Tolbert, Weaver, South, North, and East Halls
North-South Drive and Stadium Road

No new dorms had been built on campus since the late 1930s and the demand for housing was enormous. To fill this need, in the 1950s a group of dormitories were built on the west side of campus that complemented

AREA 5

VILLAGE ROAD
FRATERNITY ROW
MUSEUM ROAD
WOODLAWN DRIVE
STADIUM ROAD
NORTH-SOUTH DRIVE

1. Gator Corner Dining Center
2. Tolbert Area Residence Area
3. Apartment Residence Facility
4. 1995 Residence Facility
5. Graham-Hume Residence Areas
6. Baby Gator Nursery
7. Lake Alice, University Gardens & Bat House

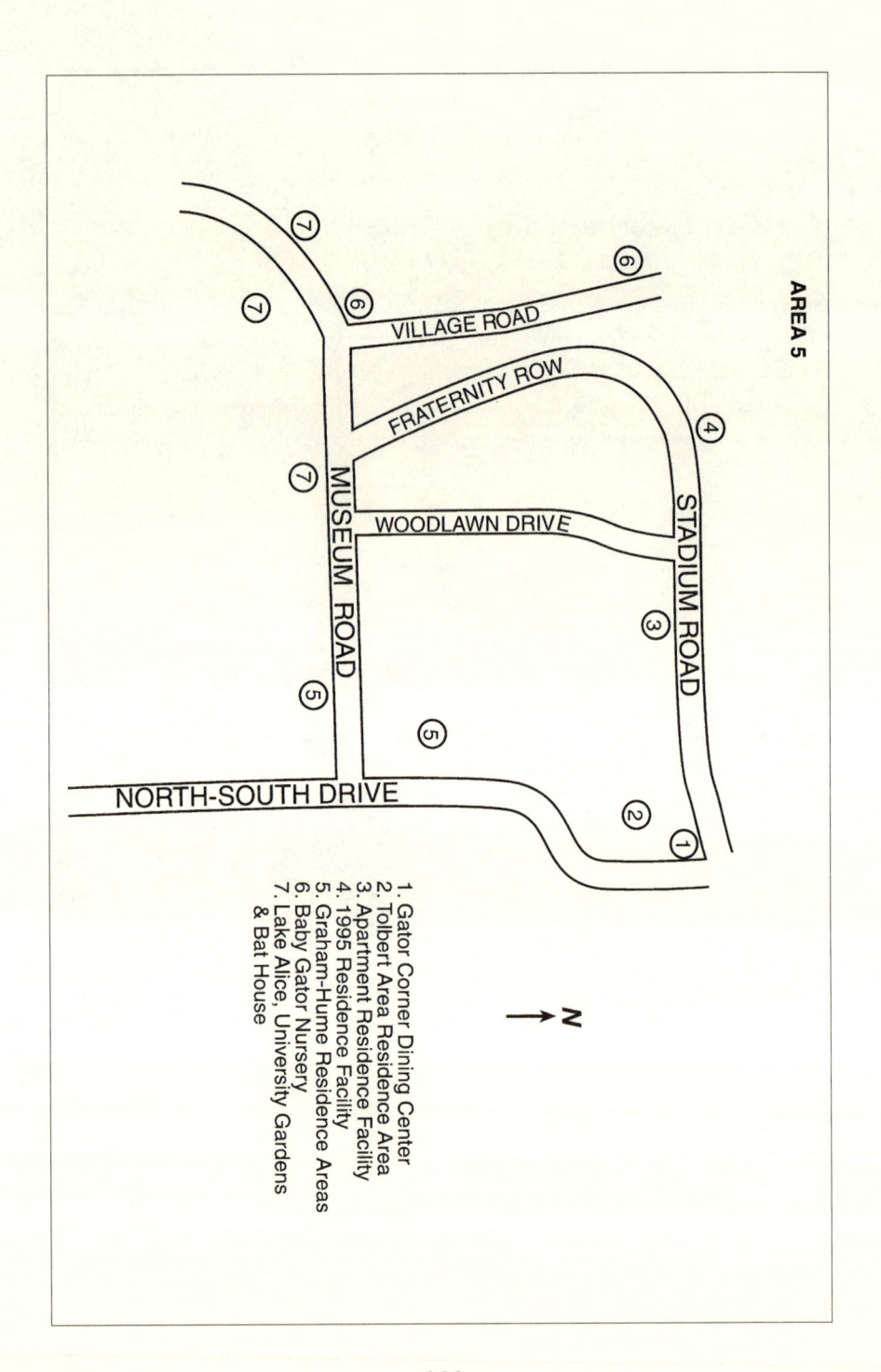

→ N

Area 5

Tolbert Area Residence Halls

the ultramodern women's residence halls built around the same time on the east side of campus.

Tolbert Hall has horizontal lines, with flat concrete awnings shading the windows and tall, glass-walled stairwells at each end. This building was named for Benjamin A. Tolbert, Dean of Students from 1929 to 1937. An adjacent residence hall in the same style is named for Martha Weaver, wife of Rudolph Weaver, first director of the School of Architecture. This dorm was first occupied by women graduate students while awaiting the completion of Broward Hall. (When UF went coed in 1947, dorms on the east side of campus were built specifically for women students and those west of the academic buildings were reserved for men, in keeping with the traditions of the time; most dorms are now coed.)

Apparently running out of names, or perhaps waiting for further significant contributions, the other three buildings in the complex are called simply South, North, and East Halls. They are located north of the Graham housing area and across the street from the O'Connell Center.

3. Apartment Residence Facility
Stadium Road

This site once bustled with the young families of World War II veterans enrolled at the University of Florida on the GI Bill, who set up housekeeping in the temporary Flavet Villages in the late 1940s. When the temporary housing was razed in 1974, the site became a parking lot. Today, the Apartment Residence Facility, a group of nine three-story brick buildings, provides 108 furnished apartments for upper division and graduate students. Each unit has four private bedrooms, a living room, two baths, and a kitchen. Each is centrally air-conditioned and heated. A community center includes laundry facilities, a computer lab, a library, a vending area, offices, and recreation rooms.

With hip and gable roofs, tall bay windows, and other traditional design features, these residences reflect an interest in recapturing the early architectural spirit of the campus. The Apartment Residence Facility is within easy walking distance of most classes and libraries, convenient to the College of Law, and just across the street from the track and field stadium.

4. 1995 Residence Facility
Stadium Road

Designed to meet the needs of the student of the 1990s, this newest residence facility features single- and double-room suites with shared baths. Not only does each furnished bedroom have telephone and cable TV outlets, but residents can access the University mainframe computers from their rooms as well. Each floor has lounges with a kitchenette and common social and recreational spaces.

Six four-story brick buildings accommodate 480 students. A common area has laundry facilities, a computer lab, recreation room, library and study center, and a vending area. This state-of-the-art student housing would amaze the young men of 1906, who moved into cramped, un-air-conditioned dorm rooms in Thomas and Buckman Halls with just one bathroom per floor. Located on the northwest side of campus, the 1995 Residence Facility is close to the O'Connell Center and the other sports facilities, as well as being within easy walking distance of the rest of campus.

The interesting octagonal shape of each building, intricate rooflines, and contrasting colors and pattern of the brickwork bring an "updated traditional" look to this new generation of student living quarters.

Area 5

Apartment Residence Facility

1995 Residence Facility

UNIVERSITY OF FLORIDA

5. Graham, Hume, Simpson, and Trusler Halls
Museum Road

When the University of Florida student population exploded in the years after World War II, on-campus housing was at a premium. To relieve some of the pressure, residence halls were built as quickly as the state could appropriate the funds and were soon filled to capacity.

In 1962, Governor Farris Bryant dedicated seven new dormitories on the UF campus. Four of them are clustered west of the main campus, not far from Fraternity Row.

Hume Hall, on the south side of Museum Road, honors Dean H. Harold Hume, a renowned horticulturist who served as Provost of Agriculture and as acting president for one month between the tenures of Presidents Tigert and Miller. Graham Hall, across the street, is named for Klein H. Graham, the UF business manager for forty-two years, beginning in 1906 when the university opened. Simpson Hall honors Thomas M. Simpson, head of the Department of Mathematics for many years and former Dean of the Graduate School. Trusler Hall is named for the Dean of the College of Law for thirty-eight years, Harry R. Trusler. Within these halls, separate sections were dedicated to other distinguished Floridians and members of the university community.

Area 5

A popular place for outdoor concerts is nearby Graham Pond, which flows into Lake Alice. In 1971, actress Jane Fonda delivered an impassioned speech against the Vietnam War to an overflow crowd gathered around this pond.

6. Baby Gator Nursery
Village Drive

The littlest Gators are nurtured in the University's Baby Gator Nursery, a childcare complex located near Corry Village Apartments and south of the College of Law. Dedicated in October of 1976, with then–U.S. Senator Lawton Chiles present at the ribbon-cutting ceremony, the facility at that time accommodated fifty-four children from ages three to five. The first two buildings were constructed with UF student funds. Admission was limited to children of UF students, filling a vital need for quality day-care for their growing families.

At present, a staff of thirteen teachers oversees the activities of over 115 youngsters. Most of their parents are students, but children of faculty and staff are also admitted as space is available.

The three cream-colored buildings that now make up the Baby Gator campus are surrounded by well-equipped playgrounds and heavily shaded by majestic pines and oaks.

Baby Gator Nursery

Child Enrichment Center
Museum Road and Village Drive

Across from Lake Alice and a short distance from the Baby Gator Nursery is the KinderCare Child Enrichment Center. The Center was built by a privately owned child-care company that has contracted with UF to provide additional on-campus facilities for the care of the young children of students, faculty, and staff.

7. Lake Alice, University Gardens, and the Bat House
Museum Road

Lake Alice, a small, shallow lake on the west side of the campus, is a favorite place to take visitors who want to see real live alligators, which can usually be viewed in the water or lounging in the sun on the small islands just offshore. The lake, which covers over one hundred acres, is an official State Wildlife Refuge and supports many aquatic and semiaquatic plants. There are also several kinds of heron, nesting osprey, gallinules, glossy and white ibis, anhingas, and turtles, in addition to the resident gators.

Lake Alice

Area 5

On the east side of Lake Alice are the University Gardens, originally developed by the Pharmacy Department as a medicinal plant garden, but now simply another pleasant place for a stroll or a quiet picnic.

Across Museum Road from Lake Alice is a curious little gray house on stilts. When bats that were nesting in the tennis stadium had to be removed, the University, in consultation with bat experts, constructed this special shelter, hoping that the bats, which need ready access to water, would like it well enough to stay. The Bat House has been pronounced a great success, and several generations of bats now help control the mosquito population and add interest to the natural attractions on the UF campus. Watching the bats stream from their house by the thousands at dusk has become a favorite local must-do.

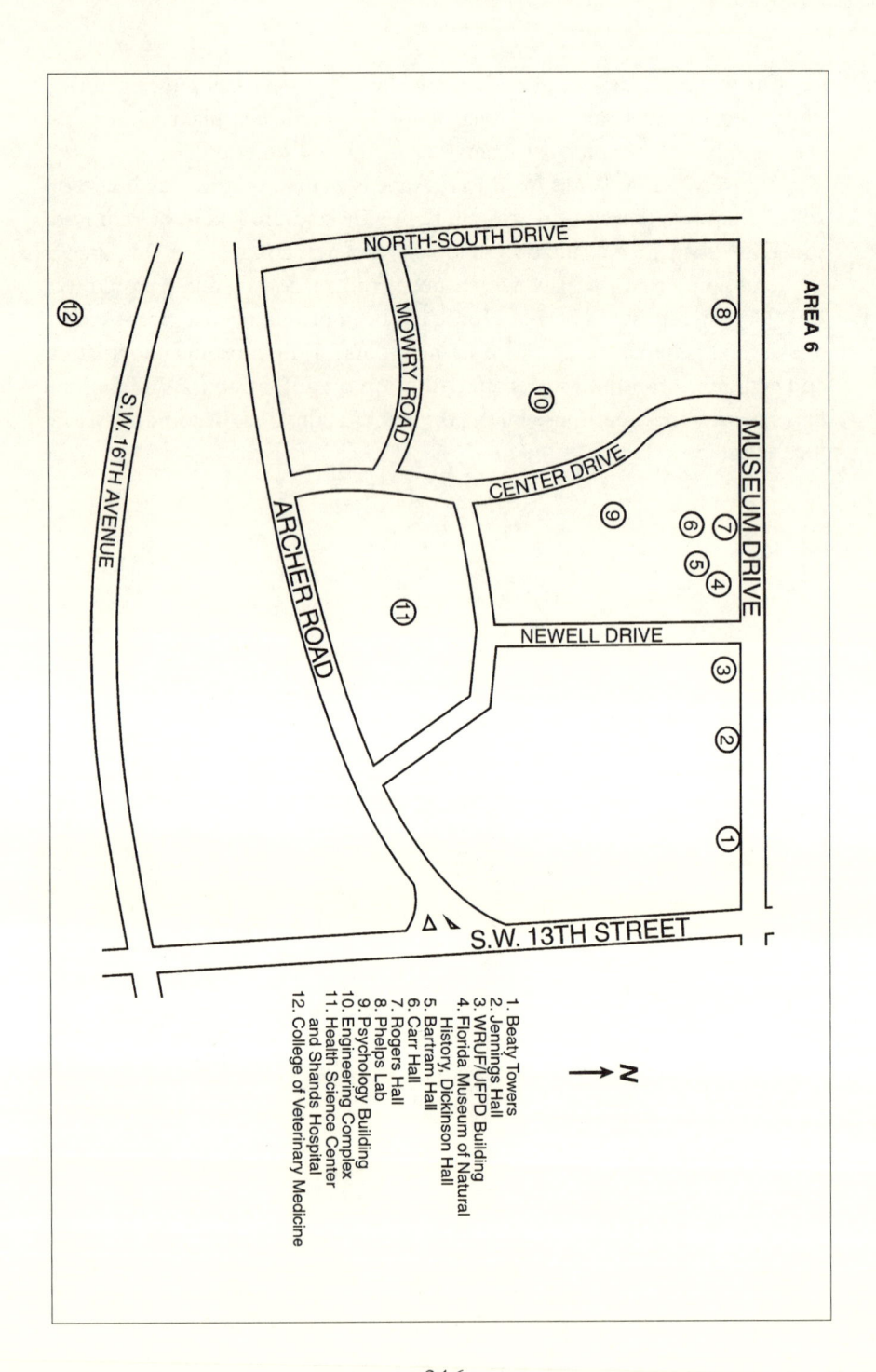

AREA 6

1. Beaty Towers
2. Jennings Hall
3. WRUF/UFPD Building
4. Florida Museum of Natural History, Dickinson Hall
5. Bartram Hall
6. Carr Hall
7. Rogers Hall
8. Phelps Lab
9. Psychology Building
10. Engineering Complex
11. Health Science Center and Shands Hospital
12. College of Veterinary Medicine

AREA 6

1. Beaty Towers
Southwest 13th Street and Museum Road

The pressing need for campus housing at the University of Florida in the 1960s compelled the construction of twin towers, one fourteen stories tall, the other thirteen stories. Instead of single and double rooms, Beaty Towers, which can accommodate up to eight hundred students, has two-bedroom apartments, each with bath, kitchen, living room, and dining room. In addition, the Towers have TV and recreation rooms, study rooms, and areas where residents can hold large gatherings, events, and parties.

Beaty Towers opened in 1966, and in 1971 was dedicated to Robert Beaty. Beaty came to UF in 1925 as the secretary of the YMCA and was a professor of sociology. In 1939 he became the Dean of Students, and when UF went coed in 1947, he became Dean of Men. Dean Beaty played a key role in pioneering student development, orientation for new students, financial aid, student government, veterans' affairs after World War II, and expansion of programs and facilities at Camp Wauburg. Regarded as a man as upright and staunch as the towers that bear his name, in 1969 Beaty was awarded the honorary degree of Doctor of Humane Letters by the University of Florida.

Beaty Towers were named after Robert Beaty, Dean of Students
Florida State Archives

2. Jennings Hall
Museum Road

Named for May Mann Jennings of Jacksonville, wife of Governor William S. Jennings, this residence hall, west of Beaty Towers and curving behind the University Police Department building, honors a distinguished Florida woman who was a pioneer in highway beautification and in the preservation of Florida's environment, particularly the Everglades.

The modern, air-conditioned facility, dedicated in 1962, was built as a women's dorm, but is now coed. It is across from the tennis courts and Broward Hall swimming pool, and has its own weight room and recreation areas.

The style of the building reflects the functional, contemporary trend in student housing that prevailed in the 1960s.

3. WRUF-UFPD Building
Museum Road and Newell Drive

The Tudor Revival building with its half-timbered walls and steep hipped roof was the original site of the campus radio station, chartered in the 1920s as WRUF, "The Voice of the University of Florida." North of the building, which was surrounded by cow pastures, were two 200-foot steel towers from which the station's antenna was suspended.

When WRUF took to the air in 1928, it broadcast weather and news, sports events, extension programs for farmers and teachers, lectures, music, and drama. This was a time for rapid progress in radio technology, and enthusiasm for the new medium was high. The station became a publicity tool for UF and a statewide medium for agricultural, governmental, and educational programs—and a training ground for future broadcasters, technicians, and communications engineers.

To build its listening audience, WRUF also featured popular programs like Red Barber's vivid play-by-play accounts of Gator sports, the Florida Farm Hour, programs for homemakers, and local gospel and country music groups. WRUF became part of the coast-to-coast Mutual Network, and many UF graduates assumed key positions in radio stations across the country.

Since 1957, when the station moved to new quarters, the building has been the headquarters of the University of Florida Police Department

Area 6

UNIVERSITY OF FLORIDA

WRUF-UFPD Building

(UFPD). The interior was renovated in the interest of efficiency in 1989, but the exterior still retains the rather quaint Elizabethan look designed by architect Rudolph Weaver. It is the only building of this style on the UF campus.

4. Florida Museum of Natural History, Dickinson Hall
Museum Road and Newell Drive

The Florida State Museum was established on the UF campus in 1917 in Science Hall (Flint Hall). The Florida Museum of Natural History, its successor, moved into this building, considered to be one of the outstanding natural history museum buildings in the country, in 1971. It is officially called the Joshua C. Dickinson Jr. Hall, in honor of its director for twenty years (1959–79).

Architect William Morgan designed the building around the concept of a Florida Indian Temple mound, with banked earth on two sides to maintain temperature and humidity levels. The Museum has public exhibition

Area 6

space on the top floor and curatorial and storage space on lower levels.

Numerous valuable collections of artifacts and specimens, including some that date back to the original museum, are available for study and used in exhibits. The Museum displays include the re-creation of a Florida cave, an oak hammock, and fossil sites. Interactive computers challenge visitors to learn more about Florida's ancient and modern flora and fauna.

Powell Hall, a new education and exhibition hall, is scheduled to open in Fall 1997 next to the Harn Museum on Hull Road. Powell Hall is designed to provide expanded space for permanent and temporary exhibits for the Florida Museum of Natural History, while the Dickinson Hall facility will continue to function as a research and teaching center.

The Museum is open to the public, free of charge, seven days a week. Phone (352) 392-1721 for information.

Florida Museum of Natural History, Dickinson Hall

5. Bartram Hall
Newell Drive

The William Bartram Biological Sciences Building was named for the distinguished eighteenth-century writer, explorer, and naturalist whose writings made the world aware of Florida's unique environment. In the 1770s this Philadelphia Quaker traveled throughout the Southeast and Florida, collecting seeds and specimens, and drawing the plants and wildlife that caught his attention. His accurate (yet poetically expressed) observations and accounts, published as the *Travels of William Bartram*, provided invaluable records of the lifeways of the Seminole Indians he met, as well as the distribution of plants and animals.

Much work is done by the faculty and students of the departments of Botany and Zoology in the field—and the forests, swamps, woodlands, coastal marshes, freshwater lakes, and saltwater habitats of Florida. However, the laboratories within Bartram and adjacent Carr Hall are essential to the deeper understanding of our environment. Here, scientists are, for example, working out the dynamics of restoring the Everglades, tracking the Monarch butterfly, and developing our understanding of the life cycles of sea urchins and wild orchids.

The contemporary brick building, completed in 1967, is built on a steep slope, and linked at its west end to Carr Hall. It overlooks the Plaza of the Florida Museum of Natural History.

6. Carr Hall
Newell Drive

Dedicated in 1989 to ecological champion Archie L. Carr Jr. (1909–87), the seven-story building with its undulating facade was completed in 1974. It houses the Carr Center for Sea Turtle Research. Archie Carr was a renowned biologist who spent his entire academic life at UF, receiving its first Ph.D. in biology in 1937. In further recognition of his far-reaching impact on the natural sciences, Carr—author, teacher, scholar, and conservationist—was selected as one of the first UF Graduate Research Professors. In addition to research and instructional labs, the building contains offices for faculty of the departments of Botany and Zoology.

The brick building has a faceted dimension, which is created by the series of bays on the south and west facades that reach from the ground to the top floor. Carr thus presents an interesting contrast to the rectangular mass of adjacent Bartram Hall.

Area 6

Carr Hall

7. Rogers Hall
Museum Road

Frazier Rogers, for whom this practical-looking building is named, was chair of the Department of Mechanical Engineering for almost forty years, until his death in 1958.

Completed in 1955, the brick structure has a two-story front section, with broad expanses of aluminum-framed windows, designed for offices and classrooms. The rear section has a saw-toothed configuration with steel beams framing the roof. Light floods in through the windows set into the spines of the roof to the open workshop below.

Tractors and other heavy farm machinery could be wheeled into this area so students could learn to apply the scientific methods of engineering to agriculture. The shop was designed for teaching farm power, drainage and irrigation, and soil conservation.

Forty years later, the building still accommodates the teaching and research mission of the department, now called the Department of Agricultural and Biological Engineering. The rear shop space has been divided into areas where such problems as the reuse of agricultural and urban waste products, post-harvest handling and preservation of food crops, irrigation management for vast greenhouse complexes, and more efficient

Rogers Hall

use of agricultural operations are under study. Students still get hands-on training and experience in how to fix a tractor engine or weld a broken farm machine, but they also learn to use computers to track weather patterns, analyze irrigation schedules, and apply satellite-generated data to soil conservation.

8. Phelps Lab
Museum Road

A handsome new addition to the front of the Phelps Lab, named for Earle B. Phelps, a professor of civil engineering (1944–53), marks the transition of this small building to its present use as the Center for Wetlands. The footbridge leading from the sidewalk to the arched entryway with its subtle bas-relief of trees is an accommodation to the sharp drop in the contour of the land. The use of red brick, the large center gable, and the stone detail above the windows and at the roofline link this sensitive adaptation to the traditional architecture of the campus.

Phelps Lab

9. Psychology Building
Center Drive

The five-story building houses teaching and research facilities for the Department of Psychology. The facade of the modern brick structure, which was completed in 1971, has an extended parapet at the roofline and a central pavilion. A flat concrete canopy defines the main entrance.

UNIVERSITY OF FLORIDA

The interior uses a modular design, which allows maximum flexibility for the inner core of laboratories and lecture rooms that can be adapted to changing needs. Faculty offices are arranged in bays on all sides of the core. Computer facilities have been expanded and updated to enable students to learn the basics of psychological research on-line. Seminar rooms and laboratories for human and animal behavioral research provide space for the study of cognition and sensory processes; comparative, developmental and experimental analysis of behavior; psychobiology; and social and counseling psychology.

Psychology Building

10. Benton, Larsen, Aerospace, Chemical Engineering, and Black Halls, and the New Engineering Building
Center Drive

Five College of Engineering buildings, clustered in a sloping area south of the J. Wayne Reitz Union, were built in the late 1960s and dedicated in 1970. Two are occupied by the Department of Electrical and Computer Engineering. These are named for John Benton, first dean of the college (1910–30), and Mervin J. Larsen, chair of the department from 1951 to 1965. Another building in the complex is the headquarters of the Department of Chemical Engineering. Adjacent to it is the home of the Department of Aerospace Engineering, Mechanics, and Engineering Science. Black Hall, the southernmost building, is the location of the Department of Environmental Engineering Sciences. It honors Alvin A. Black, a professor of chemistry and pioneer in modern water treatment practices.

These functional, contemporary buildings are all similar in design, with flat roofs, brick walls, cast concrete trim, and exposed concrete structural girders defining each floor. Multilevel landscaped terraces with brick walks and flowering trees link the buildings and form an outdoor area where students gather between classes.

Engineering Buildings

A massive new engineering building with boldly curving facades has recently been added to the complex. The two-story western portion of this facility has an auditorium and four large classrooms; offices and laboratories occupy the five-story east wing.

11. J. Hillis Miller Health Science Center and Shands Hospital
Archer Road

The University of Florida medical center is an interlocking complex of buildings, constantly evolving and expanding. Planned as a regional medical treatment center as well as a teaching and research institution, the Health Science Center was named as a memorial to UF President J. Hillis Miller after his death in 1953.

Construction began in 1955 on the Medical Sciences Building, and the College of Medicine and the College of Nursing graduated their first classes in 1960. Shands Hospital, which acknowledges the key support of Florida Senator William A. Shands in establishing the state's medical school at the University of Florida, opened in 1958. It is joined to the Health Science Center so that medical students and faculty can readily move between classrooms, clinics, labs, operating theaters, and patient rooms. The College of Pharmacy moved from its former quarters in Leigh Hall, and

The helicopter that serves Shands Hospital

the Colleges of Health Professions, Dentistry, and Veterinary Medicine were established in the next few years, each adding to the overall size and comprehensive nature of the medical center.

In 1974, the Communicore was completed, housing a library, lecture rooms, teaching labs, and audiovisual and computerized learning aids. A year later the Veterans Administration Hospital was completed across Archer Road (a tunnel under this road connects Shands and the VA Hospital).

A major renovation of Shands Hospital was completed in the late 1980s, and in 1990 two wings with sleek curving lines, enclosing a terraced courtyard, were added on the northeast end of the complex. To the east the multimillion-dollar Brain Institute is under construction.

Today over a thousand faculty teach, and more than three hundred physicians practice in the varied departments of the medical center. Many other scholars and scientists at the University of Florida also actively participate in and contribute to the research at the medical center. For example, the College of Engineering has undertaken advanced computer imagery and the development of bioglass, and the Arts in Medicine program functions in collaboration with the departments of Art, Music, and Theatre and Dance.

12. College of Veterinary Medicine
Southwest 16th Avenue

One of the most appealing features of the University of Florida campus are the several fields where horses calmly graze, oblivious to the passing traffic or the relentless expansion of the University's building program. Most of these horse fields are in the vicinity of the College of Veterinary Medicine on the south rim of the campus. One of the finest new features of the College is the Alec and Louise Courtelis Equine Teaching Hospital, which opened in 1994. Owners of one of the nation's premier Arabian horse breeding farms, the Courtelis family has been very supportive of the work of the College of Veterinary Medicine for many years. The hospital, which supplements existing facilities, has an expanded surgery suite, free-standing isolation and reproduction barns, and state-of-the-art equipment. A new academic building, opened in 1996, adds administrative, classroom, and research space to the College. The steel pipes visible at the roof are air

UNIVERSITY OF FLORIDA

College of Veterinary Medicine

handlers, part of the facility's ventilation system. They emphasize the functional purpose of the modern structure, which contains small- and large-animal surgery teaching labs, thirty-eight research laboratories for faculty use, and the latest teaching and computer support systems for students.

AREA 7

1. Harn Museum of Art
Southwest 34th Street and Hull Road

Symbolizing the University's continuing commitment to the fine arts is the Samuel P. Harn Museum of Art, which opened in 1990. The contemporary museum offers a full range of programs—films, lectures, guided tours, workshops—and performances—for the general public as well as the academic community. One of the three largest visual arts facilities in Florida, it is also one of the largest university art museums in the nation. It is spacious enough to host major traveling art shows as well as its growing permanent collection.

Designed by UF alumnus Kha Le-Hue, the building is a stunning asymmetrical arrangement of curves and angles, of smooth stuccoed exterior walls detailed by bands of travertine marble and blocks of granite, an intricate roofline and soaring glass and metal facades. At the entrance, the fountain bridge passes over the shimmering stone mosaic "Fragmented Reflections" by Jim Piercy. The interior draws in an abundance of natural

Samuel P. Harn Museum of Art

AREA 7

S.W. 34TH STREET

BLEDSOE DRIVE

MUSEUM ROAD

HULL ROAD

NO-NAME ROAD

ARCHER ROAD

SURGE AREA DRIVE

① ② ③ ④ ⑤ ⑥

N →

1. Harn Museum of Art
2. Center for the Performing Arts
3. Southwest Recreation Center
4. Entomology & Nematology Building
5. Fifield Hall
6. Microbiology & Cell Science Building

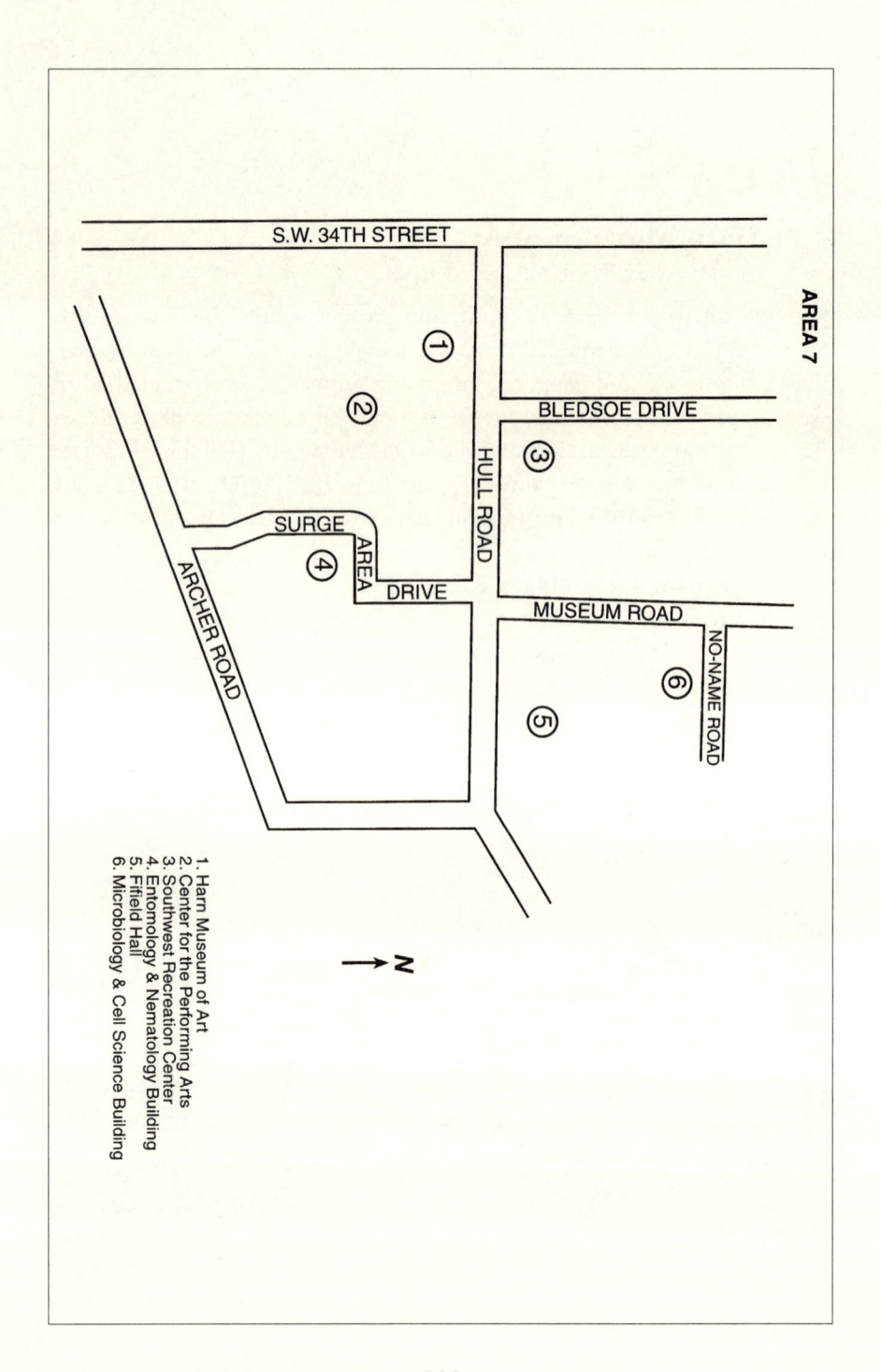

Area 7

light from many sources—the "witch's hat" of the tetrahedron above the sixty-foot-high rotunda, walls of windows in the lobby, skylights, and interior garden courts open to the sky.

Space flows easily, leading the visitor from gallery to gallery. While there is always something new to see around the corner, works from the permanent collection can be viewed and appreciated over time like good friends.

The Harn Museum was made possible by a gift of the Harn family and honors Samuel P. Harn, who managed the Gainesville Chamber of Commerce for many years. Along with the adjacent Center for the Performing Arts and Powell Hall, the Florida Museum of Natural History's new education and exhibition center, the Harn forms part of an exciting cultural complex on the western edge of the campus.

2. Center for the Performing Arts
Hull Road

The Center for the Performing Arts officially opened in January 1992 with the professional touring company's performance of *Cats*. The state-of-the-art facility seats eighteen hundred people in the main auditorium and has a smaller "Black Box" theater for experimental works.

The main stage is fifty feet wide with a depth of forty-eight feet, and the proscenium arch is thirty-two feet high. Thus, the Center can accom-

Center for the Performing Arts

modate the scenery and extensive personnel of lavish Broadway productions, complete orchestral and choral groups, fully staged ballets and operas, as well as more modestly staged productions. The "sprung" stage is kind to dancers, and stage technicians appreciate the double-purchase fly system for hanging scenery and lights.

The design of the building and its interior decor are simple and classical, relying on neutral colors and the subtle repetition and rhythm of circles and squares. The structure has a modern flair in its symmetrical design with a curved roofline, an entrance canopy suspended by two massive braces attached high on the facade, and a circular fountain in front.

Planned as a regional performing arts facility, its year-round calendar includes classical music, popular artists, professional dance and theater companies (both touring and those based in the area), magicians, folk singers, ethnic performers, and much more. It is part of the cultural complex just off Southwest 34th Street that includes the Harn Museum of Art and Powell Hall. For information about programs and tickets, call (352) 392-2787.

3. **Southwest Recreation Center**
Hull Road

Strong horizontal lines are emphasized in the tricolor patterns of the brick on the facade of this modern recreation building, part of a larger complex of playing fields set on twenty-six acres on the southwest corner of the campus. The main entrance is an expanse of glass, framed with red brick and topped with an octagonal dome. Tall palms set along the front emphasize the design created by the alternating colors of brick, and the octagonal theme of the dome is repeated in the front sidewalk and in the front entry hall. A set of sneakers with green laces is the whimsical theme of the abstract colored-glass mural over the front entrance.

Within the 60,000-square-foot fitness facility are courts for basketball, racquetball, volleyball, and other sports; strength equipment and activity rooms for aerobics classes and the like; and lockers and showers. There is even a rock-climbing wall for the ultimate fitness test. The adjacent fields and park include four lighted softball diamonds, ten tennis courts, and three basketball courts. A new stadium for the UF women's softball team anchors the southeast corner of the complex.

Area 7

Southwest Recreation Center

Entomology and Nematology Building

UNIVERSITY OF FLORIDA

4. Entomology and Nematology Building
Hull Road and Surge Area Drive

Located off Hull Road, east of the Center for the Performing Arts, is the Department of Entomology and Nematology, part of the College of Agriculture. The one-story building of light tan brick, surrounded by an earthen berm, is distinguished by the tubular corrugated metal that sets off the roofline. A central lobby and an atrium display evidence of current research on insects and their interactions with man. An enclosed garden patio is planted with a variety of butterfly-attracting flowers and shrubs.

Across from the Entomology and Nematology Building is a natural wetlands area used as a teaching lab for environmental studies.

5. Fifield Hall
Hull Road

Constructed in 1979 but not dedicated until 1982, Fifield Hall honors horticultural scientist and administrator Willard M. Fifield, who directed the Agricultural Experiment Station for fourteen years (1941–55) and served as provost for agriculture for seven years (1955–62).

Fifield Hall is headquarters for the departments of Horticultural Sciences, Environmental Horticulture, and Plant Pathology and contains

Fifield Hall

offices, classrooms, computer facilities, and laboratories. Greenhouses and plots adjacent to the building allow for controlled environment and field studies. Faculty and students in these departments also carry out horticultural research in fourteen centers throughout the state, from Homestead to Quincy.

6. **Microbiology and Cell Science Building**
Museum Road

The secret life of cells is under intensive investigation in this modern facility, located south of Lake Alice. The one-story brick building features flaring metal canopies over the entrances and main facades. Laboratories within the building are equipped to unravel the mysteries of the smallest organisms on earth, the bacteria, cells, and viruses that so powerfully affect the growth and development of plants and animals. The Department of Microbiology and Cell Science, a division of the Institute of Food and Agricultural Sciences (IFAS) and part of the College of Agriculture, moved into this handsome structure in 1994.

Microbiology and Cell Science Building

HERE AND THERE

1. President's Mansion
University Avenue

The official residence of the University of Florida's president was completed in 1953, sited on a ten-acre triangle of land north of the main campus. The university architect, Jefferson Hamilton, designed the Neocolonial building with a formal entrance, a stately portico with four columns, which opens to the reception hall and the other rooms on the first floor designed for entertaining large groups. Florida-made brick and timber contributed by the UF School of Forestry were used in the construction.

An informal patio area with swimming pool and a footbridge over a small stream are located in the rear of the building, in an area framed with natural landscaping.

The mansion was completed in time for the university's centennial celebration in 1953, and President J. Hillis Miller and his wife received thousands of alumni and friends who came to Gainesville for the celebration. Since then, each University of Florida president's family has occupied the official home and has graciously entertained the thousands of visitors who come to the mansion.

2. Fraternity and Sorority Houses

The tradition of locating residence halls for men on the west side of campus and those for women on the east side extends to a large degree to UF fraternity and sorority houses. Fourteen of the twenty-nine UF fraternities have houses located near the College of Law on Fraternity Row, which was established in the 1950s, and eleven of the eighteen sororities built houses along Panhellenic Drive, east of Southwest 13th Street and south of Norman Hall. Each building has its own architectural style, and most are embellished with symbols of the organizations.

Fraternities have been active on campus since UF was founded, and much of the social life of the University centered around these organizations. However, until sororities were established on campus in 1947, frater-

HERE AND THERE

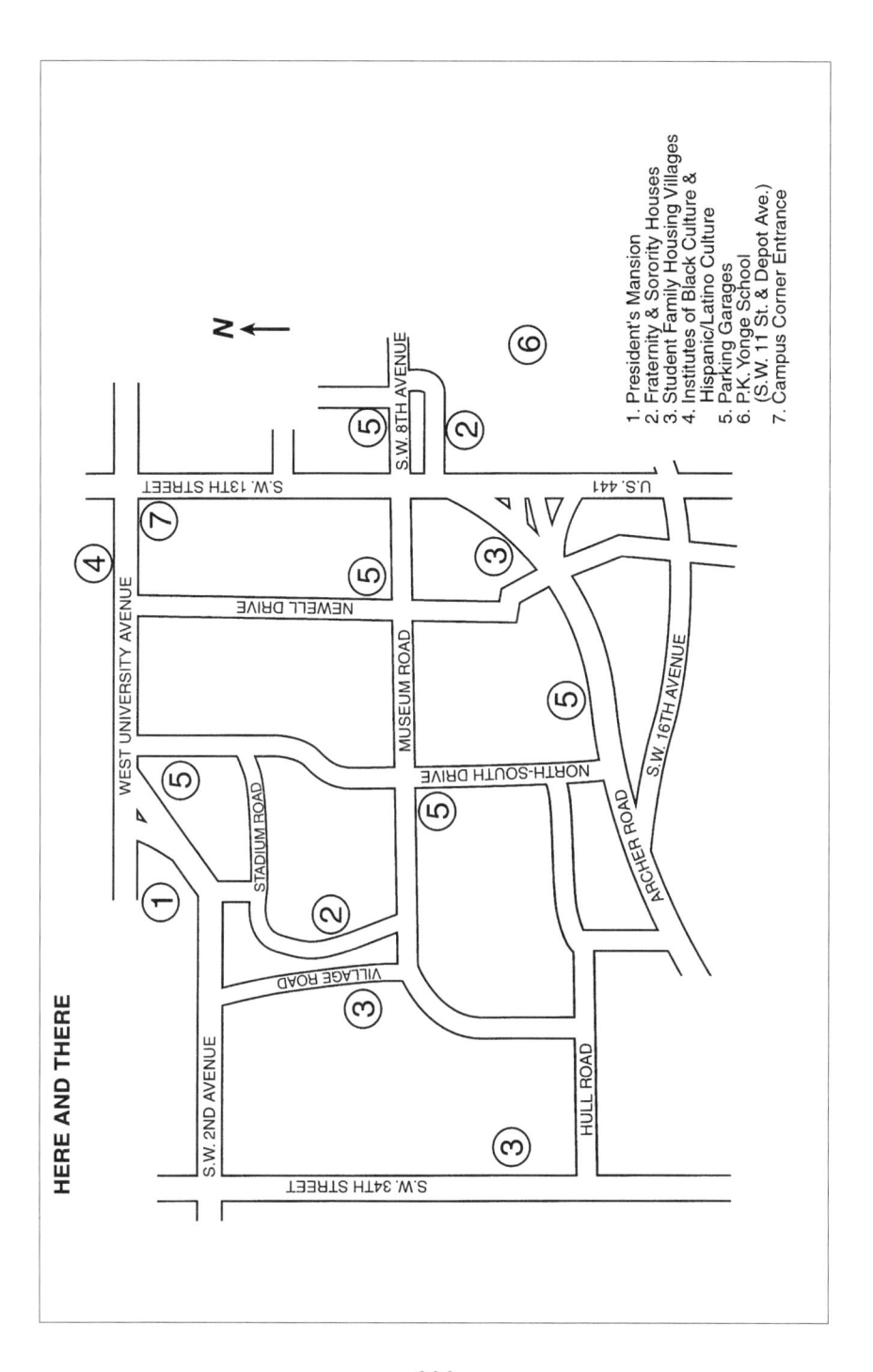

1. President's Mansion
2. Fraternity & Sorority Houses
3. Student Family Housing Villages
4. Institutes of Black Culture & Hispanic/Latino Culture
5. Parking Garages
6. P.K. Yonge School (S.W. 11 St. & Depot Ave.)
7. Campus Corner Entrance

239

UNIVERSITY OF FLORIDA

President's Mansion around 1960

Florida State Archives

Chi Omega Sorority House in 1961

Florida State Archives

nity men either invited young ladies from the Gainesville community or "imported" them from afar for their parties, picnics, and dances.

The following fraternities belong to the UF Interfraternity Council: Alpha Epsilon Pi, Alpha Gamma Rho, Alpha Phi Alpha, Alpha Tau Omega, Beta Theta Pi, Chi Phi, Delta Chi, Kappa Alpha, Kappa Alpha Psi, Kappa Sigma, Lambda Chi Alpha, Omega Psi Phi, Phi Beta Sigma, Phi Delta Theta, Phi Gamma Delta, Phi Kappa Tau, Phi Sigma Kappa, Pi Kappa Alpha, Pi Kappa Phi, Pi Lambda Phi, Sigma Alpha Mu, Sigma Chi, Sigma Nu, Sigma Phi Epsilon, Sigma Pi, Tau Epsilon Phi, Tau Kappa Epsilon, Theta Chi, and Zeta Beta Tau.

The Panhellenic Council is comprised of the following sororities: Alpha Chi Omega, Alpha Delta Pi, Alpha Epsilon Phi, Alpha Kappa Alpha, Alpha Omicron Pi, Alpha Xi Delta, Chi Omega, Delta Delta Delta, Delta Gamma, Delta Phi Epsilon, Kappa Alpha Theta, Kappa Delta, Kappa Kappa Gamma, Phi Mu, Pi Beta Phi, Sigma Gamma Rho, Sigma Kappa, and Zeta Tau Alpha.

3. Student Family Housing Villages

Following World War II, so many veterans returned to school accompanied by wives and children that the University had to erect temporary (and very spartan) housing very quickly (some of it surplus military barracks). The residents formed their own governing bodies in the various Flavet (short for Florida veterans) villages and tried to help one another survive the difficulties of combining family life with student life.

The last Flavet buildings were demolished in the early 1970s. By then married students were accommodated in family housing villages, modern apartment complexes complete with laundry facilities, playgrounds, recreational facilities, and other amenities. Because many of the village residents are graduate students who come to the University of Florida from all over the world, these communities have a lively international flavor.

Corry Village opened in 1959 and is named for William W. Corry, UF student body president in 1942–43 and captain of the varsity football team, who gave his life for his country in World War II. Maguire Village, which opened in 1972, is named for Raymer F. Maguire, another UF student body president (1915), a College of Law graduate, and a dedicated UF alumnus. Diamond Village is named for Emery Gardiner Diamond, also a former UF student body president, who was killed in a plane crash.

Student Family Housing Villages

4. Institute of Black Culture and Institute of Hispanic/Latino Culture
University Avenue and Southwest 14th Street

A pair of two-story frame houses on University Avenue, directly across from Anderson Hall, are headquarters for programs and activities for two of the University of Florida's diverse ethnic student groups. Built early in the twentieth century as family homes and later used as boarding houses for UF students, the buildings still retain their dignified and comfortable homelike ambiance.

The Institute of Hispanic/Latino Culture, called "La Casita" by the students who gather here, is a home away from home for UF's Hispanic and Latino students. It provides comfortable lounges, conference rooms, with original art on the walls, a media and reading room, and a place for a wide variety of groups to meet and mingle.

The Institute of Black Culture is very similar in appearance, with the exception of the second-story front porch, which has been enclosed to provide space for the institute's library. Conference rooms, lounges, and offices welcome students who want to learn more about our Black Culture and participate in the social and cultural programs provided by the Institute.

Here and There

Institute of Black Culture

5. Parking Garages

Parking is one of the perennial problems on the University of Florida campus. In the campus plan of 1906, the place of the automobile was not considered. The interior streets on campus were not paved until the 1930s, and they had to be realigned to match those of the surrounding Gainesville streets. Historic photographs in the 1920s and 1930s show only a few cars parked in front of the buildings.

By the 1950s and 1960s campus roads were widened and parking lots appeared. Eventually, most traffic was banished from the center of the campus, at least during class hours, to create a pedestrian- and bicycle-friendly environment.

The latest answer to the increase in the number of cars on campus has been the construction of a series of parking garages. One, a structure with steep Gothic gables, is located south of Norman Hall. Another one near the Florida Museum of Natural History's Dickinson Hall has alternating bands of brick and concrete, indicating that when the parking garages were designed, the prevailing architectural styles on campus were taken into consideration. There are additional parking structures near the O'Connell Center, on North-South Drive, and several in the Health Center complex.

One of the several parking garages on campus

6. P.K. Yonge Developmental Research School
Southwest 11th Street and Depot Avenue

The P.K. Yonge Laboratory School was established in 1934 as a model school for the UF College of Education. It was dedicated to training Florida teachers as well as developing and testing new and more creative teaching methods.

Until 1958, the K–12 facility was housed in what is now Norman Hall, the home of the College of Education. At that time, a new campus for P.K. Yonge was created on a wooded site through which Tumblin' Creek meanders, about five blocks southeast of the main UF campus.

The school, which has a current enrollment of over seven hundred, has developed a familylike community on its campus of rambling one-story brick buildings and emphasizes individualized, quality education, while continuing to serve as a demonstration school for the College of Education.

Now called the P.K. Yonge Developmental Research School, the institution was named for Philip Keyes Yonge, who was a member of the State Board of Control when UF was founded, and who served on the Board for twenty-eight years.

P.K. Yonge Developmental Research School

UNIVERSITY OF FLORIDA

7. The Official Campus Corner Entrance
University Avenue and Southwest 13th Street

A gift of the Class of 1951, the diagonal brick wall on the corner of University Avenue and Southwest 13th Street marks the northeast corner of the campus. On the wall is a bronze plaque depicting the University of Florida seal and words written in 1950 by UF President J. Hillis Miller, beginning, "Our state and Nation will always need men and women who perform justly, skillfully, and wisely. . . ."

FURTHER READING

The material used as background for writing about the buildings on the University of Florida campus came from many sources. For the benefit of readers who want to know more about these buildings, the following resources are suggested:

The Florida Alligator 1910–73. After February 1973, it became the *Independent Florida Alligator* (an index is available in the University of Florida Library).

The Gainesville Sun (an index is available in the Alachua County Main Library in Gainesville).

Historic Preservation Projects in the collection of the Architecture and Fine Arts Library, University of Florida.

Samuel Proctor and Wright Langley. *Gator History: A Pictorial History of the University of Florida.* South Star Publishing Company, Gainesville, FL, 1986.

The Seminole (UF Yearbook, 1910–73) (not published 1974–82).

The Tower (UF Yearbook, 1983 to date).

University of Florida Archives in Smathers Library, University of Florida.

INDEX

Boldface entries refer to photographs

A

1995 Residence Facility 210, **211**
A. Quinn Jones Center 89
Academic Advising Center 166, **167**
Acrosstown Repertory Players 59
Adkins, James 81
Adkins, Shelton "Red" 81
Aerospace Engineering Building 227
Agricultural Experiment Station 169, 170, 200, 236
Alabama Street 98
"Alachua" (French Fries from Hell) 190
Alachua Army Air Base 86
Alachua Avenue **6**, 20, 21, 26
Alachua County Abstract Company 23, 69
Alachua County Administration Building 32
Alachua County Medical Society 60
Alachua County Museum and Archives 16
Alachua County Public Library **15**, 16, **17**
Alachua County School Board 20
Alachua General Hospital 41, **62**, 98, 99, 110
Alachua Hotel 55
Alachua Lake 114, 115
Alachua Medical Society 21
Alachua Sink 114
Alachua Steam Navigation and Canal Company 24
Alachua Volunteers Investment Corporation (Alavic) 47
Alfred A. Ring Tennis Pavilion 182, **183**
Altrusa House 110
Alvarez Tourist Home 21
American Legion Building 16
American Legion Post Number 16 16, 49
American Waterworks Landmark 49
Anderson, James Nesbitt 150
Anderson Hall 139, 144, **149**, 150, 242
Anderson Memorial Organ, Dr. James 136
Apalachicola 20
Apartment Residence Facility 210, **211**
Archer 61, 103
Archer Road 26, 60, 114, 119, 120
Architecture Building 186
Arlington Hotel 100
Arlington Square Apartments 10, 43
Arredondo, Don Fernando de la Maza 3, 199
Arts in Medicine 229
Askew, Reuben 146
Association of American Universities 133
Atlantic Coast Line (ACL) Railway 41, 67
Atlantic, Gulf and West India Transit Railroad 65
Austin, Elizabeth 44
Austin, Oliver 44
Austin Ornithological Research Station 44
AvMed Santa Fe 62
Ayer, A.B. 94
Ayers, Orien 98
Ayers, R.V. 111

B

B'Nai Israel Jewish Center 64
Baby Gator Nursery **213**
Badgers 84
Bailey, James 31, 99
Bailey, J.B. 23
Bailey House **99**
Baird, Eberle 34, 39, 45
Baird, Emmett 45
Baird Hardware 39, 45, 59
Baird Hardware Company Warehouse 59
Baird House-Magnolia Plantation **45**
Baird Theater 34, 39

249

Baird Theatre-Cox Building 34, **35**
Baker family 20
Banks, Cullen W. 98
Baptists 61, 108
Barber, Red 194, 218
Barnes, Louis 34
Barnes Building 34
Barracks Park 75
Barrow, Mark and Mary 24, 26, 41, 44, 86
Bartlett, Don 194
Bartram, William 3, 222, 115
Bartram Hall 222
Baseball 65, 84
Bat House 214, 215
Batey, Hal 44
Battle of Gainesville 22, 97
Bear, Fred 119
Beard, Percy 180
Beaty, Robert **217**
Beaty Towers 107
Bed-and-breakfasts 21, 29, 45
Ben Hill Griffin Stadium at Florida Field **176**
Bennett, Charles 146
Benton, John 227
Benton Hall 138, 140, 195, 227
Bethel Gas Station 35, **36**
Beville, E.F. 56
Bivens Arm Nature Park **114**
Black, Alvin 227
Black Hall 227
Blanding, Albert 73
Blanding House 73, **74**
Bless Auditorium, Arthur A. 193
Board of County Commissioners 23
Bodiford, James 72
Bodiford, Mary Jesse 73
Bodiford House 72, 73
Bostick Club House, Guy 184
Boulware Springs 31, **48**, 49, 114
Boyd family 81
Bradford County 15
Bradford County Courthouse 118
Brechner Center for Freedom of Information, Joseph L. 194
Broward, Annie 203
Broward, Napoleon B. 203

Broward Hall 203, 209, 218
Brown Cottage 83
Brubeck, Dave 105
Brush, Charles 92
Bruton, Judge James D. and Mrs. 184
Bruton-Geer Hall 184
Bryan, Nathan P. 146
Bryan, William Jennings 77, 78
Bryan Hall 146, **147**
Bryant, Farris 212
Bryant Space Sciences Center, Thomas **168**
Buchholz, F.W. 111
Buchholz, Mrs. F.W. 112
Buchholz Junior-Senior High School 118
Buck, William 62
Buckman, Henry 161
Buckman Hall 131, **160**, 161, 210
Burr, Aaron 7
Burtz Printing 53
Business Building 146, **147**
Butler, Neil 89

C

Calkins, Sande and Keifer 90
Calloway, Cab 96
Camp Blanding 46, 73, 96
Career Resource Center 199
Carillon 134, 136
Carl Perry Baseball Diamond 178, **179**
Carlton, William G. 141
Carlton Auditorium 141
Carnegie Corporation 15
Carr, Archie 222
Carr Hall 222, **223**
Carter, Jr., Vernon T. 111
Cato's Store 91, 95
Cedar Key 7, 60, 65, 72
Center for African Studies 138
Center for Latin American Studies 138
Center for the Performing Arts **233**, 234, 236
Center for Wetlands 225
Central City Nine 65, 84
Century Tower 133, **134**, 154, 190
Chamber of Commerce 23
Chapin House **90**

Index

Charles L. Blount Downtown Center 118
Charles, Ray 171
Chase, Charles 82
Chemical Engineering Building 227
Chemistry Laboratory Building 157, 158
Chemistry Research Building 157, 158
Chestnut, Cynthia 89
Chestnut III, Charles 89
Child Enrichment Center 214
Chiles, Lawton 146
Citizens Alliance 94
Citizens Field **84**
Citrus 5, 8, 19, 29
City alderman 22
City Commission 14
City council 14, 23, 56
City Furniture 55
City Hall **14**, 15, 56, 108
City Park 75
City seal 22, 97
Civil War 5, 8, 22, 63, 65, 75, 87, 92, 97, 103
Clock tower **13**
College of Agriculture 156, 170, 189, 200, 236, 237
College of Architecture 186, 189
College of Arts and Sciences 150
College of Dentistry 221
College of Education 139, 205, 206, 245
College of Engineering 138, 140, 194-96, 227, 229
College of Fine Arts 186, 189, 190
College of Health and Human Performance 173, 175
College of Health Professions 229
College of Journalism and Communications 194
College of Law 81, 146, 182, **183**, 184, 210, 213, 238
College of Liberal Arts and Sciences 154, 160, 166, 167, 168
College of Medicine 228
College of Nursing 228
College of Pharmacy 157-58, 228
College of Veterinary Medicine 229, **230**
Collegiate Gothic 133, 143, 148, 160, 161, 163, 166, 170, 173, 191, 206

Colson, B.R. 23
Colson, James 21
Colson family 20
Commercial Hotel 55, **57**
Community Plaza **38**
Computer and Information Science Building 190, **191**
Congregation B'Nai Israel 63
Constans, Philip 198
Constans Theater 198
Copland, Aaron 190
Corry, William W. 241
Corry Village 213, 241
Cortelis, Alec and Louise 229
Cosby, Edgar 94
Cotton 5, 29, 60, 99, 100
Court of Two Sisters 39
Courthouse **5**, 8, 10, 13, 31, **32**, **33**, 43, 51
Courthouse Square 10, 29, 31, 32, 48, 50
Cox Furniture Company Warehouse **58**
Cox Furniture Store 35
Crawford, Ben 25
Crawford Tourist Lodge 25
Criser, Marshall M. 144
Criser Hall 139, 144, **145**
Crom, Ted 13
Cushman, Alonzo 21
Cushman–Colson House **21**
Cypress Inn Billiards 53

D

Daily Sun newspaper 50, 53
Dairy Science Building 201, **202**
Dance Alive! 112
Danscompany 112
Dauer, Manning J. 166
Dauer Hall **166**, 198
Davis, Horatio 73
Davis, Isaac 92
Davis Livery Stable 56
de Soto, Hernando 3
DeBose, E.H. 111
Dell, George 44
Dell, Jr., S.T. 112
Depot Avenue 49, 64
Desert Storm 120

Devil's Millhopper **116**
Diamond, Emery Gardiner 241
Dickinson, J. C. 220
Dickinson Hall 220, 244
Division of General Extension 107
Division of Sponsored Research 138
Dixie Hotel 24, 107
Doig, James 22, 23, 49
Doig Cotton Gin 100
Doig Foundry and Machine Works 22
Doig House 22, 23
Dorsey's Funeral Home 91
Downtown Plaza 32
Duck Pond 79-82
Durrance, Mattie 25
Durrance, Oscar 25
Durrance House **25**
Dutton, H.F. 103
Dutton Bank 21, 100
Dutton Bank Building 100, **102**

E

East Florida Seminary 8, 15, 70, 75, 156
East Hall 207, 209
Eastern Airlines 86
Eastside Elementary 19
Eastview subdivision 46
The Eden of the South 97
Edwards, Heidi 166
Edwards, J.F. 34
Edwards, William 82
Edwards, William A. 82, 134, 136, 140, 149, 150, 163
Edwards Hospital 62
Edwards Opera House 34
Eldred, Dale 144
Emerson Courtyard, William and Jane 146, 147
Endel, Moses 63
Engineering Building 227
Entomology and Nematology Building **235**, 236
Episcopalians 61
Epworth Hall 70, **71**, 72, 75
Everglades National Park 73
Evergreen Cemetery 49, **50**, 58, 73

F

Fagan House 41
Fagan's Shoe Store 41
Fager, Charles J. 158
Farmer's Journal 103
Farr, James 80, 81
Farr–Adkins House 80, **81**
Feliciano, Jose 105
Ferandino, Andrew 189
Fernandina 7, 50, 65
Fernandina–Cedar Key Railroad 7, 8, 31, 65
Fifield, Willard M. 236
Fifield Hall 236
Fifth Avenue Arts Festival 95
Fine Arts Complex 186, **188**
Finger, W.L. and Mike 31
Fire chiefs 21, 56, 77
Fire department 14, 56
Fire Station No. 1 14, 56, **57**
First Advent Christian Church 72
First Baptist Church **108**
First Christian Church 108
First Federal Savings and Loan 25
First Presbyterian Church 60, **61**
First United Methodist Church 72
Fisher School of Accounting, Frederick and Patricia 146
Fitzgerald, Ella 96
Flanagan, Alvin G. 194
Flavet 210, 241
Fleming Field 175
Flemington 61
Fletcher, Duncan U. 162
Fletcher Hall 161
Flint, Edward R. 160
Flint Hall 131, 139, 158, **159**, 220
Florida A&M University 103
Florida Agricultural College 150, 162, 169
The Florida Alligator 139, 143, 166, 175
Florida Annual Conference 92
Florida Blue Key 149
Florida Conference of the United Methodist Church 109
Florida Farm Colony 21

Index

Florida Federation of Women's Clubs 109
Florida Field 176, 177
Florida Gators 133, 176
Florida Gym(nasium) 171, 173
Florida legislature 19, 82, 118
Florida Medical Association 41
Florida Museum of Natural History 44, 220, **221**, 222, 233, 244
Florida National Bank 34
Florida Normal College 103
Florida Players 198
Florida Railroad 65
Florida Railway and Navigation Company 65
Florida Senate 21, 50, 103
Florida Southern 97
Florida State League 84
Florida State Museum 13, 107, 158, 160
Florida State Pharmaceutical Society 73
Florida State University 78
Florida Theatre 35, 104, **105**, 106
Florida Union 166
Florida's Environmentally Endangered Lands Program 117
Florida's House of Representatives 103
Floyd, H. 98
Floyd, Wilbur L. 156
Floyd Hall 139, **156**, 200
Fold's Hardware Store 34
Fonda, Jane 213
Fordyce, Joseph 118
Fowler, James 23
Fowler House **23**
Fraternity Houses 238, 239
Fraternity Row 212, 238
Fred Bear Museum **119**
Freedman's Bureau 8, 87, 92
Freedom 87
Friends of the Library 109
Friendship Baptist Church 91, **92**
Frost, Robert 83, 136
Fulton, Guy 141, 195, 204

G

G-Men 84
Gaines, Edmund Pendleton **7,** 8, 31
Gainesville Academy 8, 75
Gainesville Ballet Theatre 112
Gainesville Chamber Orchestra 112
Gainesville Chevrolet Company 39, 53
Gainesville Civic Chorus 112
Gainesville Community Playhouse 110, **112**
Gainesville Gas 98
Gainesville Graded and High School 19
Gainesville Guards 50
Gainesville Guards Armory 100
Gainesville High School 111, 112
Gainesville Little Theater 112
Gainesville Lodge 41 (Masons) 67
Gainesville National Bank Building 100, **102**
Gainesville Public Library 15
Gainesville Regional Airport 86
Gainesville Sun 42, 84
Gainesville Symphony Orchestra 112
Gainesville Woman's Club 15, 109, **110**, 112
Gannett Auditorium 194
Garrison, Bessie Marie 94
Garrison Nursery School 94, **95**
Gator Bumpers 106
Gator Corner Dining Center 207
Gehan, Clara and Freddie 81
Gehan House 81
Georgia Seagle Hall 109
Gibbons, Sam 146
Glee Club 132, 190
Glover and Gill Grocery 96
Gordon, Buff 14
Gordon, Ulysses S. "Preacher" 61
Gorrie, John 20
GPA (General Purpose A Building) 154
Gracy, Luther 76
Gracy House **76**, 77
Graduate School 138, 144, 149, 150, 212
Graham, Klein 77, 212
Graham Hall 212
Grandmother's Park 66
Grant, Ulysses S. 100
Gray, Henry 44
Gray, L.M. 46, 85

253

Gray, Lucian 46
Gray House 46
Great Southern Music Hall 104, 105
Green Cove Springs 109
Griffin, Ben Hill Jr. 156, 157, 176
Griffin-Floyd Hall 156, 157
Grinter, Linton 138
Grinter Hall 138, 140
Grove Street 94
Gulf of Mexico 7

H

H.F. Dutton Company 100
H.F. Dutton Phosphate Company 103
H.M. Chitty & Co. 34
Hague 72
Haile Plantation 118
Haisley Lynch Gardens 58
Hamilton, Jefferson 144, 238
Happy Hour Billiards 53, **54**
Hardee, Cary 136
Hare Krishnas 152, 153
Harn, Samuel T. 221, 231, 233
Harn Museum of Art 221, 231, 233
Harris, Charlie 84
Harris Field 38, 84
Hav-a-Tampas 84
Hawthorne 15, 49, 114
Hawthorne Road 28, 42
Haymans, Joseph 34
Health Science Center 228, 229
Henry, John 190
Heritage Club 107
High Springs 15
Highlands 85
Hill Printing Company 21, 55
Hillel Foundation 64
Hippodrome State Theatre 42, **43**
Historic Gainesville, Inc. 73, 83
Hodges, James 41
Hodges House **40**, 41
Hogtown 7, 8
Holbrook, Hollis 150
Holbrook family 73
Holland, Georgia Seagle 109
Holland, Spessard L. 146, 182

Holland Hall 182
Holy Trinity Episcopal Church 14, 41, 70, **71**
Honeycutt, Bethel 35
Hope, Bob 171
Hope Lodge 110
Horseshoes 103
Hotel Thomas 82, 118
Howard, Andrew 24
Howard House–Kelley Lodge **24**
The Hub 191, **192**
Hume, Harold 212
Hume Hall 212
Hunt, Donna 98
Hurston, Zora Neale 150

I

I(nterstate)-75 118, 120
IFAS (Institute of Food and Agricultural Sciences) 200, 201, 237
Imperial Hotel 55
Indian mound 184
Infirmary 173, **174**
Ingram, Tilman 31
Institute of Black Culture 242
Institute of Hispanic/Latino Culture 242, **243**
Institute of Inter-American Affairs 152
The Islands 106

J

J. Hillis Miller Health Science Center 228
J. Wayne Reitz Union **198**, 199
Jacksonville 103
Jacksonville Beach 80
Jennings, Ed 89
Jennings, May Mann 218
Jennings, Waylon 105
Jennings Hall 218
Jester family 77
Jewish Synagogue **63**
Johnson, Lyndon 173
Johnson Brothers 53
Johnson Hall 91, 166
Jones, A. Quinn 89
Joseph Williams Elementary School 46

Index

Josiah Walls Historical Marker 103
Judicial Center 32

K

Kanapaha Botanical Gardens **120**
Kanapaha Church 60
Kanapaha Park 120, **121**
Kelley, McKee 24
Kelley Hotel 107
Kelly Power Plant 49
Kennedy, John F. 173
Kincaid Road 49
King, T.F. 23
Kirby Smith Chapter 32
Kirby Smith School 19, **20**
Knight Courtyard, John S. and James L. 194
Krugman-Kadi, Eilon 25
Ku Klux Klan 91

L

Lady Gator athletics 180
Lake Alice 213, **214**, 215, 237
Lake City 77, 78, 80, 82
Language Hall 149
Larsen, Mervin J. 227
Larsen Hall 227
Le-Hue, Kha 231
Leigh, Townes R. 157
Leigh Hall **157**, 158
Lewey, Matthew 103
Lewis, William 31
Lewisville 31
Liberty Street 16
Library Association 15
Library East 150, 152
Library West **151**, 152
Lillian's Music Store 39
Lincoln Grill 96
Lincoln High School 47, 96, 111
Lincoln Middle School **47**
Lincoln Theater 95, 96, 105
Little, Winston 142
Little Hall 141, 142
Loblolly School 81
The Lodge 24, 25

Loften, W. Travis 26
Lone Star 106
Long, Rodney 89
Lynch, Haisley 16, 49, 58
Lynch, Louis 58
Lynch, Mary Helen 58
Lynch Park 58

M

Magnolia Plantation Bed and Breakfast Inn 45
Maguire, Raymer F. 241
Main Street Cocktail Lounge 55
Mallory, Angela 205
Mallory, Stephen 205
Mallory Hall 204
Manchester, Melissa 105
Marshall, Jean and Terry 23
Marston, Robert Q. 190
Marston Science Library 190
Martin Luther King, Jr., Monument 14
Martin Luther King Jr. Multipurpose Center 84
Masonic Lodge 103
Masonic Temple 67, **69**, 70
Masons 67
Material Science and Engineering Building 196, **197**
Matherly, Walter Jeffries 148
Matherly Hall 146, 148
Matheson, Alexander 19
Matheson, Augusta 50
Matheson, Christopher 19, 50
Matheson, James Douglas 50
Matheson, Sarah Hamilton 19
Matheson Historical Center 16, **18**, 19, 91, 110
Matheson House **18**, 19
Matthews, D. R. "Billy" 166
McArthur, A.J. 77
McArthur, John 56
McArthur–Graham House 77
McCarty, Dan 200
McCarty Hall 200
McCormick, William 60
McCreary, H.H. 50, 53

McGill family 82
McGinley, James 137
McGurn, Ken and Linda 43
McKenzie, Reed 20
McKenzie House 20
McKethan, Alfred A. 179, 180
McKethan Stadium, Alfred A. 178, **179**
McQuown, Ruth O. 168
Mechanical Engineering Building 140, 196, **197**
Melton Motors 53
Methodists 61, 72, 109
Metz Theatre 91
Micanopy 15, 60, 61
Microbiology and Cell Science Building 237
Microkelvin lab 193
Mike's Bookstore and Tobacco Shop 39
Miller, J. Hillis 85, 132, 158, 228, 238, 246
Millhopper Road 115, 117
Missionaries 3
Monteocha 87
Moore, Henry, "The Archer" 152
Mordock, Mrs. Hal 112
Morgan, William 220
Morningside Nature Center 26, **27**, 28
Mount Pleasant Cemetery 111
Mount Pleasant United Methodist Church 91-**93**, 94, 111
Mucozo Tower 163, **164**
Murphree, Sr., Albert Alexander 78, 80, 82, 136, **139**, 163
Murphree, "Waddie" 82
Murphree Hall 163
Murphree House 78, **79**
Music Building **189**, 190
Myers, Gardiner and Jane 73

N

Nation, Carry 76
National Guard Bureau 73
National Register of Historic Places 19, 29, 37, 49, 58, 59, 64, 79, 83, 92, 107, 133, 165
Naylor, Geoffrey 138, 186

Neighborhood Housing and Development Corporation 66
Nelson, Willie 105
Neuharth Library, Allen H. 194
New Baird Building 39
New Era 103
New York Giants 175
Newell, Wilmon 170
Newell Hall 160, 169, 170
Newins, Harold S. 200
Newins-Ziegler Hall 199
Newnan, Daniel 28
Newnans Lake **28**
Newnansville 7, 31, 65
Nichol's Alley 106
Nicholoson, L.A. (Nick) 56
Nixon, Richard 173
Norman, James W. 206
Norman Hall 139, 205, 206, 238, 244
North Florida Regional Medical Center 62
North Hall 207
Northeast Historic District 70-86
Nuclear Sciences Building 195-**197**

O

Oak Halls 84
Oakley, Stephen C. 184
Oaks Mall 6
Ocala 60, 70
Official Campus Corner Entrance 246
Old Mount Carmel Baptist Church 91
Olmsted, Frederick Law, Jr. 132
Olympics 180, 182
Orange Creek 61
Ortiz, Juan 163
O'Connell, Stephen C. 136, 171, 177, 178

P

P.K. Yonge School 112, 139, 245
P.K. Yonge Library of Florida History 152
P.M. Stafford's Office 91
Pancoast and Associates 191
Parker, Julia 94
Parker, Julius A. 94, 98, 111

Index

Parker Drug Company 94
Parker–Cosby House 94
Parking Garages 139, 244
Parrish, M.M. 85
Paynes Prairie 3, 4, 24, 49, 114, **115**
Peabody Hall 139, 144
Peninsular and West India Transit Company 65
Pepper Printing Company 53, 55
Pepper Publishing Center 42
Percy Beard Track and Field Complex 180, **181**, 182
Perry, Carl "Tootie" 180
Peter, Paul, and Mary 171
Petty, Tom 105
Phelps, Earle B. 225
Phelps Lab **225**
Phifer family 20
Phosphate 5, 8, 19, 29, 82, 103
Piercey, Jim 194, 231
Pithlachoco 28
Plant, Henry 97
Plaza of the Americas 139, 152
Pleasant Street 91, 95
Pleasant Street Historic District 87, 92
Pleasant Street Historical Society 91
Plummer's Barber Shop 95
Porter, O.A. 65
Porter, Watson 34, 65
Porter Building 34
Porter–Haymans–Woodbridge Building 53
Porter's Community Center 66
Porter's Oaks 66
Porter's Quarters 65
Post office 42, 53, 84
Pound family 20
Powell Hall 221, 233
Presbyterians 60, 61
President's Mansion 238, **239**
Primrose Inn and Grill 104
Primrose Square **104**
Prohibition 76
Psychology Building 224, **225**

R

R. Scott Linder Tennis Stadium, 182
Racquet Club 173
Raff, Marcia 174
Railroad Depot **64**, 97, **98**
Railroads 5, **11**, 29, 97, 98
Rails-to-trails 49, 114
Rancho de la Chua 3
Rat caps 131
Rawlings, Marjorie Kinnan 136, 150, 203
Rawlings Hall **202**, 203
Reconstruction 95
Regional Transit System 35
Reid, Mary Margaret 205
Reid, Robert R. 205
Reid Hall 204
Reitz, J. Wayne 198
Reitz Union 166, 196, **198**, 199
Revolutionary War 3, 120
Rice Hardware 59
Richards House 72
Richenbacher's 55
Rickenbacker, Eddie 55
Rinker School of Building Construction, Marshall E. 186
Rion, William E. 198
Robb, Robert 60
Robb, Sarah 60
Robb House 60
Robertson, Alan 118
The Rock **154**
Rogers, Frazier 224
Rogers Hall 224
Rolfs, Peter H. 170
Rolfs Hall 170
Ronald McDonald House 110
Roosevelt, Teddy 100
Roper, James Henry 75
Roper Park **75**
ROTC 178
Rural Resettlement Division 14

S

S.B. Duke's Saloon 55
Salvation Army 25, 26

Samaritan Hotel 55
San Felasco Hammock State Preserve **117**
San Francisco de Potano 117
Santa Fe Community College 83, 98, **118-19**
Santa Fe Junior College 42, 118
Santa Fe Regional Library 15
Savannah, Florida and Western Railroad 55, 56, 97
School of Forestry 200, 238
Science Hall 131, 158, 220
Scott Linder Tennis Stadium 182
Scruggs, Carmichael Building **33**, 34
Seaboard Coast Line Railway 41, 65
Seagle, Georgia 107
Seagle Building 24, **107**
Seagle Furniture Store 59
Second Advent Christian Church 72
Second Seminole War 4, 7, 117
Seminary Street 95
Seminole Hotel 55
Seventh Day Adventist 72
Shands, William A. 228
Shands Hospital 62, 173, 228, 229
Shaw and Keeter Ford Building **106**
Simpson, Thomas M. 212
Simpson Hall 212
Skeeter's 106
Sledd, Andrew 162
Sledd Hall 161-**64**
Smathers, George 148, 150
Smathers Library 150, **151**, 152
Smith, Edmund Kirby 19
Sorority Houses 238-41
South Carolina Annual Conference 92
South Garden Street 103
South Hall 207
Southeast Historic District 29-50
Southwest Recreation Center 234, **235**
Sovereign Restaurant 39, **40**
Spring Pilgrimage 79
Standard Crate Company 45
Star Garage 36, **37**
Starke 73, 118
Statuary Hall 19

Steinbrenner, George 180
Stephen C. O'Connell Student Activity Center 171, **177**, 178, 182, 207, 209
Stud's Pool Hall 53
Student Family Housing Villages 241, **242**
Student Health Care Center 173
Student Recreation and Fitness Center 173, **174**
Sun Center 42
Sunland 21
The Swamp 176
Swearingen, Thomas 43
Swearingen Auto Company 44
Swearingen–Austin House 43, **44**
Sweethearts of Rhythm 96
Sweetwater Branch 7, 16, **17**, 26, 29, 79, 80
Sweetwater Branch Inn 21

T

Tabernacle 16
Tacachale 21
Teaching Zoo 119
Tebeau, Margaret "Maggie" 50
Telegator 144
Tench, Benjamin 53, 55
Tench, J. Dawkins 55
Tench Building 53, **54**, 55
Tennis 182
Third Regiment 87
Thomas, Thomas Fraser 69
Thomas, William R. 82, 163
Thomas Center 77, 82, **83**
Thomas dairy barn 80
Thomas Hall 82, 131, 160, 162, 163, 169, 210,
Tigert, John J. 80, 85, 86, 132, 143, 152
Tigert Hall **143**
Tigert House **85**, 86
Timucuans 3, 4
Tipton family 78
Tolbert, Benjamin A. 209
Tolbert, Margaret Ross 198
Tolbert Hall 207, **209**
Tomkies, J.H. 108
Tower Road 120

Index

Transit line 97
Treaty of Paris 3
Trusler, Harry R. 212
Trusler Hall 212
Tumblin' Creek 65
Tung oil 9, 53
Turlington, Ralph 154
Turlington Hall 154, 170
Twentieth Century Club 15, 109
Tyree, Larry 118

U

U.S. Congress 103
UFPD (University of Florida Police Department) 218, **220**
Uggams, Leslie 111
Union Academy 8, 65, 87, 89, 91, 92, 94
Union County 15
Union Street Entertainment District 11
United Daughters of the Confederacy 32
United States Land Office 34
United States Tung Oil Laboratory 53
University Athletic Association 166, 180
University Athletic Association Athletic Center 180, **181**
University Auditorium 34, 132, 136, **137**, 138, 152, 154
University Boulevard 16
University College 141, 142
University Furniture Company 55, 59
University Gallery 186
University Gardens 214, 215
University Golf Course 184, **185**

V

Van Fleet, James A. 178
Van Fleet Hall 178, **179**
Veterans Administration Medical Center (VA Hospital) 26, 62, 229
Victoria Square Apartments 41
Vidal, James 79
Vidal's Lake 79
Vietnam War 111, 213
Volleyball 180

W

W. Travis Loften Center 26, **27**
Wabash Hall **96**
Wacahoota 61
Waldo Road 38, 47, 63, 84, 86, 89, 114
Walk Through Time 120
Walker, E. S. 140
Walker Hall 140
Walls, Josiah 89, 103
Walter's Blue Room 95
Walton, John 175
War of 1812 7
Warren, Earl 184
Warriner, Bill 78
Warrington, Alfred 148
Warrington College of Business Administration 146-48
Warrington Fine Interiors 90
Wayside Press 53
Weaver, Martha 209
Weaver, Rudolph 157, 161, 162, 163, 186, 201, 209, 220
Weaver Hall 207
Weber, Carl 97
Weed, Edwin 70
Weil, Joseph 195
Weil Hall 194, **195**, 196
Weimer, Rae O. 194
Weimer Hall 192, 194
Wesleys 72
West Florida Seminary 78
West Union Street 29
Westside Park 8, 84
White–Jones Funeral Home 69, 91
White House Hotel 72, 80
White's Hotel 55
Williams, Dick 69
Williams, Joseph 46
Williams Hospital 62
Williams-Thomas Funeral Home 69
Williamson, J. D. 192-93
Williamson Hall 192-93
Windsor School of Learning 45
Wise, Sr., Joe 106
Wise's Drug Store 106

259

Women's Gymnasium 175
Woolworth Building 63, 100
Works Progress Administration 94
World War I 5, 16, 49, 53, 55, 58, 73, 95, 132, 173, 177
World War II 6, 16, 29, 46, 86, 96, 107, 132, 134, 160, 165, 178, 194, 210, 212, 217, 241
WRUF-UFPD Building 218
WUFT-TV 84

Y

Yellow fever 50, 63, 97
Yon, Everett 82
Yon–Murphree House 82
Yonge, Philip Keyes 245
Young Men's Democratic Club 91
Yulee, David Levy 7, 8, 205
Yulee, Nancy Wycliff 205
Yulee Hall 204

Z

Zellar, Eloise 112
Ziegler, Edwin A. 200